Presented to

....

By

....

Date

....

DEVOTIONS TO QUIET *Your Soul*

DEVOTIONS TO QUIET *Your Soul*

COMFORTING INSPIRATION FOR WOMEN

JANICE THOMPSON

BARBOUR
PUBLISHING

Print ISBN 979-8-89151-193-4

Published by Barbour Publishing, Inc., 1810 Barbour Drive, Uhrichsville, Ohio 44683, www.barbourBooks.com

Our mission is to inspire the world with the life-changing message of the Bible.

Member of the Evangelical Christian Publishers Association

Printed in China.

Introduction

You long for peace and stillness but wonder if you will ever find it in this crazy, rush-about world. Every time you try to settle yourself, something interferes. The boss. The kids. Social media. You can hardly get your bearings before someone or something is tugging at you. Will you ever catch a break?

God wants you to know that right here—even in the chaos—it's possible to find rest for your soul. Even on the craziest day, when you're ready to throw in the towel, you can walk in supernatural peace. God's Word is filled with verses that will calm your troubled soul and help you every step of the way.

If you struggle to find rest, this devotional was written just for you! Filled with 180 inspiring readings, *Devotions to Quiet Your Soul* touches on topics that are sure to encourage and uplift you, always pointing you toward the one who gives rest. If that seems impossible, read on. Within the pages of this book you will find the biblical truth you need to settle your heart, mind, and soul in your heavenly Father's comforting embrace.

Rest: A Gift from God

"Come to me, all who labor and are heavy laden, and I will give you rest. Take my yoke upon you, and learn from me, for I am gentle and lowly in heart, and you will find rest for your souls. For my yoke is easy, and my burden is light."
MATTHEW 11:28–30 ESV

Have you ever considered the notion that rest is a gift from God? No, it doesn't come wrapped in ribbons and bows, but it's a present from Him all the same, a "kick your feet up and take it easy" offering straight from a heavenly Father who knows what it's like to work, work, work.

You know too. You're diligent, a hard worker who rarely takes time off. Sometimes it's easier to keep going than to give yourself time and space for your body, soul, and spirit to recover.

But they're desperate to recover. That body of yours wasn't meant to go 24/7, 365 days a year. Remember, God even gifted Himself a day of rest—He was leading by example when He created the Sabbath.

Like any gift, this one has to be opened. Think of those presents under the Christmas tree when you were a kid. Did you just leave them sitting there or dive in to tear back the paper? Of course you dove in!

It's time to tear back the paper, girl. Give yourself permission to rest. Heaven knows, you need it.

I need rest, Lord. Desperately. I'm worn out. Thank You for the gift of rest. Today I choose to open the gift and learn from Your example. Amen.

He Makes Me Lie Down

He makes me lie down in green pastures,
he leads me beside quiet waters.
PSALM 23:2 NIV

Cora wasn't one to rest. As a high-powered executive, she was expected to keep things running at the company. But when she came down with the flu, everything came to a grinding halt.

And yet, somehow, the company survived. Actually, other people kicked in and did the work necessary to keep things running like a well-oiled machine. Cora didn't see her illness as a gift, but she had to admit the truth of that "He makes me lie down in green pastures" verse she'd grown up quoting. After all, what other choice did she have when she was so sick?

Maybe you've been in a similar situation. You didn't want to stop, but something—a family situation, an injury, an illness—painted you into a corner. There you were, completely at a standstill. Frustrated. Confused. But after a while you saw the downtime for what it really was: a gift.

We don't celebrate troubles. But we do see that God can make good from what the enemy meant for evil. Our heavenly Father can turn our trials into a season of rest. At times that's exactly what we need.

Lord, I'm going to look at even the hardest of times as a blessing. You can turn what the enemy meant for evil into a season of rest for me. I'm counting on You, Jesus! Amen.

Fan Rest to Flame

For this reason I remind you to fan into flame the gift of God, which is in you through the laying on of my hands.
2 TIMOTHY 1:6 NIV

This is a fascinating verse from Paul to Timothy. The great apostle is encouraging young Timothy, who's still on a learning curve, to "fan into flame" the gift that is within him.

Maybe you know what that's like—you've had to fan some gifts into flame in your own life. You worked hard to develop your gift as a singer, a dancer, a writer, a cook, a mom. You learned how to be a good employee, solid in your knowledge of what was expected of you. It didn't come naturally, but after a while you developed some serious skills.

Though this may seem counterintuitive, that's how it is with rest too. God wants you to fan this gift into a flame. Work hard to make yourself rest! It won't come naturally. You'll want to keep going, doing the work that never seems to get done. But fan this gift of rest into a flame that leads you straight to the sofa. Or to bed. Or to your prayer closet.

Don't overlook rest as a spiritual gift. It's yours for the taking... so take it.

Lord, thank You for the reminder that I'll need to keep fanning this gift into a flame if I'm to claim it. May I never forget that godly rest is a true gift—from You to me. Amen.

Under Warranty

God's gifts and God's call are under full warranty—
never canceled, never rescinded.
ROMANS 11:29 MSG

Have you ever purchased a warranty for something—say a car? Then, a few days after the warranty expired, the car broke down? Happens all the time. . .

Sue experienced this frustration when she bought a new dishwasher for her condo. At the salesman's urging, she purchased a top-of-the-line unit—and the warranty, as well.

Unfortunately, less than a month after the warranty expired, so did the dishwasher. Turned out it was way too expensive to have the parts replaced, so Sue ended up buying a new one. This time she went with a cheaper model and was disappointed.

We've all been there in one way or another. But that's what makes today's verse so great. God's gift of rest? It's under full warranty. It's not going to expire. He'll never cancel it, never rescind it. This gift is meant to last your whole life. God never says, "Hey, this week I'll restore your soul, but next week? You're on your own, kid!" Nope, He's got you, on good days and bad, in busy seasons and calmer times. You can trust Him to take great care of your soul, sister.

Thanks for covering me, Lord! I'm grateful Your gifts
come with a money-back guarantee! Amen.

Open the Gift, Girl

Thanks be to God for his inexpressible gift!
2 CORINTHIANS 9:15 ESV

While on a lunch date with her best friend, Trina was given a birthday gift. Bess told Trina not to open the present until she returned home. On her way out of the restaurant, Trina stuck the gift in the trunk of her car. . .and forgot all about it!

A couple of days later Bess texted: "Well? What did you think?"

"About what?" Trina responded.

Several minutes went by before Bess replied, "My gift. Didn't you think it was perfect? I was hoping it would touch your heart."

Trina went into panic mode, racing to her car and grabbing the package from the trunk. Back inside, she opened the box to discover the cutest ceramic dachshund, a perfect replica of her little Sasha, who had recently passed away. How thoughtful of Bess to offer such a gift. Trina felt like a heel for completely forgetting it.

Can you picture God, the ultimate gift giver, looking down from heaven, saying, "Girl, are you ever going to take advantage of what I've already given you? I offered you peace. I gave you rest. And yet you left them in the trunk!"

Open His gift of peace and rest today. You'll be so glad you did.

Thank You for the reminder to open Your gifts,
Lord! You're the best gift giver ever! Amen.

For Many Were Coming and Going

And he said to them, "Come away by yourselves to a desolate place and rest a while." For many were coming and going, and they had no leisure even to eat.

Mark 6:31 ESV

You know how it is. You wish you had time to yourself, but whether it's kids, your husband, coworkers, or friends, you're rarely alone. Take another look at today's verse in light of the many, many people in your world. Getting away? It's tough on a good day. But on a hard day, a chaotic day, it seems impossible to go away by yourself to a desolate place and rest.

Sure, it sounds great. . .just out of the question.

God certainly knew what it would be like for you. He's not asking the impossible. And He wouldn't give a command if He didn't plan to help you fulfill it.

So what does it look like to slip away? Here's how Dahlia did it: Once a week she snagged a couple of hours just for herself. She picked up her favorite coffee at the drive-thru, then headed for a nearby lake where she settled in at a picnic table with a good book. These breakaways accomplished two important things—they got her out into the sunshine (vitamin D, you know) and provided some desperately needed separation from the day-to-day routine.

Maybe you need a respite too. Many are coming and going in your world and you'd like to escape them, if only for a moment. Make your plan, then follow through!

Show me how, Lord. Show me where. And show me when! I'm keen to slip away for a few hours. Amen.

Strive. . .to Rest

Let us therefore strive to enter that rest, so that no one may fall by the same sort of disobedience.
Hebrews 4:11 ESV

"What do you mean, I have to work to rest?" Sharen was perplexed by the notion as she stared into her husband's concerned eyes.

"I'm just saying it doesn't come naturally to you," he countered. "I know how you are, honey. You're like the Energizer Bunny. You wear yourself out. So for you to rest is going to require something of you. That's why I'm pushing so hard for us to get away, to go on this vacation together. I think a few days in the mountains will do you good."

"With no internet?"

"Exactly. And limited access to phone service too."

"Sounds dangerous."

"Sounds heavenly." He gave her a look. "And once you settle in, I think it'll sound pretty amazing to you too."

Maybe you're like Sharen. Resting sounds like work. You find it hard to be still, to break away from the chaos. But look again at today's verse: God instructs us to *strive* to enter rest. That's a command. It's also a command with a valuable reward attached. Don't miss out.

I'm ready, Lord! I'll work hard. . .to rest in You. Amen.

No Fear in Resting

Where God's love is, there is no fear, because God's perfect love drives out fear. It is punishment that makes a person fear, so love is not made perfect in the person who fears.

1 John 4:18 NCV

Some people can't seem to settle down and rest because of fear. Their thoughts tumble around in their heads nonstop, replaying all that's gone wrong—and all that could possibly go wrong.

During these times, it's important to remember how much you are loved. Once you experience God's incredible love, you'll figure out that it's worth the effort to "try" to rest. (Yep, you really have to *try*!)

Gillian had a lot of fear and anxiety. She blamed herself for pretty much everything and had a hard time letting go. But with time and effort, prayer and Bible reading, she finally released herself from the unforgiveness she felt toward herself. And then the power to rest came. Gillian was finally able to put her head on the pillow and drift off to a peaceful sleep.

Maybe you need to do some hard work now so that you can eventually have a restful outcome. It will be worth it. Ask God to help you get to the bottom of what troubles you. Then turn it over to Him completely. You'll finally experience true peace and rest.

I get it, Lord. I have to do the hard work so that I'm finally free to relax and just be. I'm tired of blaming myself for things, for worrying and fretting. Help me to power through all the "whys" so I can reach Your peaceful place. Amen.

Everything You Do or Say

Everything you do or say, then, should be done in the name of the Lord Jesus, as you give thanks through him to God the Father.
COLOSSIANS 3:17 GNT

Some days you're just not feeling it. You don't want anyone to remind you that Christians "shouldn't act that way." And you definitely don't feel like drawing close to God. You'd rather stay upset, thank you very much. Those are actually the days when you need God most, and when it's more critical than ever to pull away from the chaos and spend time with Him.

Today's scripture is a clear indicator that everything—yes, everything—should be done with the Lord in mind. What you say. What you do. Where you go. Who you hang out with. How you respond. How you don't respond. What you spout in anger. What you think in your heart. It's all with (and for) *Him*.

Ouch. There are days when you just can't imagine behaving well, right? Rebellion mode makes it hard to focus on anything other than your own situation. But God, in His wisdom, commands you to shift your focus.

Look to Him. Look *at* Him. Seek His perspective, His words of healing, His rest.

When your mind and heart are held by the one who loves you most, the tension in your body begins to drain away. And best of all? You can change the outcome of your day. Yes, it's possible!

I'll shift my focus, Lord. I'm done being rebellious and upset. I want to do things Your way, but I'm definitely going to need Your help. Amen.

He Sees You When You're Sleeping

You see me, whether I am working or resting; you know all my actions.
PSALM 139:3 GNT

Remember when you were a kid, how you tried to get away with things, hoping your parents wouldn't find out? They usually did anyway.

We haven't changed much, have we? We act one way in front of our friends and family. Sometimes they might even think we're hyperspiritual. But, in the secret places? Not so much.

Here's the thing: God sees. He knows when we're struggling. He knows when we're faking it. He knows when we're hoping no one else recognizes the issues we're battling. And He adores us anyway.

You know that funny Christmas song about Santa: "He sees you when you're sleeping, He knows when you're awake. . ."? Of course that's not true. But those exact words can be used to describe God. He really does see when your head is on the pillow. And He knows the anxieties and struggles you face when you're awake.

Your heavenly Father really does know when you've been bad or good. . .but His affection for you isn't based on your behavior. You don't get gifts under the tree for being good. You get all of God, no matter what, just for the asking.

Father in heaven, thank You for loving me in spite of my flaws. You see it all, Lord, and love me anyway. How grateful I am! Amen.

Why Do I Toil?

It is in vain that you rise up early and go late to rest, eating the bread of anxious toil; for he gives to his beloved sleep.
PSALM 127:2 ESV

Annie paced her kitchen, phone in hand. "Why am I killing myself?" she groaned.

"Good question," her best friend responded.

"I mean, I work around the clock to pay the bills, but I'm so tired that there's no time left over to really enjoy anything—people, places, or things. It's kind of a blur."

"You do move pretty fast," Callie agreed.

"What choice do I have? There are bills to pay, the mortgage company is breathing down my neck. . .all important stuff."

"Yes," Callie replied, "but maybe it's time to pare back some of your activities and slow your roll."

Annie laughed. "Slow my roll?"

"Yeah, that's what the kids say. But you get my point. Maybe it's time to let a few things go so that you're not so wound up all the time. You know?"

Annie did know. And maybe you know too.

It's time, girl. Time to let a few things go. Those added obligations that aren't helping you. Neither is all the extra stuff—and its accompanying debt. It's time to revamp, restructure, and reexamine everything. Why? So you can rest.

Please help me examine my obligations, Lord. Check my heart and my motivations, I pray. Amen.

A Hard Task

"People have a hard task on earth,
and their days are like those of a laborer."
Job 7:1 NCV

"People have a hard task on earth." Maybe you read those words and groan. You've found it to be true. Everything seems hard—your job, your family, even your friends at times. No matter which way you turn, you run into some difficult thing.

Megan felt this. She and her husband struggled with their mortgage payments. Then she made a mistake with her debit card and overdrew their account. There was the strain of her daughter's health problems. And that coworker who always tried to one-up her.

On and on the troubles went. It seemed every day was filled with trials, morning to night. Megan couldn't settle her heart and mind, during the workday or in the evenings at home, which should have been a refuge.

Maybe you're like that too. Troubles overflow, spilling onto everything. When life just seems too hard, remember Job, who had the hardest story of all. In the end, God redeemed every bit of it. In His own time and way, God will redeem your story as well. Consciously put your trust in Him, and God will even bring peace in the midst of your storm.

I'm so tired of everything being hard, Lord.
Help me through these storms, I pray. I'm ready to
put my trust in You so that I can be refreshed. Amen.

The Sweat of Your Brow

"You will have to work hard and sweat to make the soil produce anything, until you go back to the soil from which you were formed. You were made from soil, and you will become soil again."

Genesis 3:19 GNT

Maybe you've heard the expression "Life is hard, but God is good." It's so true! From the moment Adam and Eve blew it in the garden, when they fell prey to that slippery serpent, humankind has been on a sweaty old hamster wheel that never stops. Many work from sunup till sundown, falling exhausted into bed late at night. Maybe you're one of them.

God never intended His beloved to live like this. His plan for Adam and Eve was to walk with Him in the cool of the evening. To drink in His presence. To rest, contented, in Him.

But they messed up big-time. Adam and Eve allowed sin into the world—and it brought its nasty cousin, toil, along with it. So instead of strolling with God in the cool of the day, most of us are slaving away just trying to pay the bills.

But God longs for us to lay aside our sweaty pursuits—to wipe our brows and come to Him. There is still rest for the weary. It's found in the presence of our Savior, who paid the ultimate price to redeem us.

Lord, I'm so grateful that You give rest to the weary. Thank You for providing rest to counteract my sweat! Amen.

Shine That Light, Girl

"In the same way your light must shine before people, so that they will see the good things you do and praise your Father in heaven."
MATTHEW 5:16 GNT

Most people think of today's scripture as an evangelism message. . .and it is. God wants you to shine your light to spread the gospel. But there are other (lovely) benefits of shining bright for Him. For instance, we lead others by example. They see the things we're doing right and want to emulate us.

Now think about that as it pertains to rest. Your kids are watching, Mama. Your sisters in Christ are looking on. Your husband, your boss, your coworkers, your neighbors. . .everyone is picking up cues from *you*. What are they learning? To work around the clock? To keep go-go-going, even to the point of exhaustion? Sure, your boss might like that (and take advantage of it), but you're teaching others that wearing yourself out is the best way to go.

It's not. So teach a different lesson. Lead by example in *rest*. Show the people around you how to chill. . .how to say no. . .how to put your feet up. . .how to skip the get-together so you can take a nap. Teach them that spending time with your heavenly Father is a lot better than making sure you're the toast of every party. In short, lead by example, girl!

Lord, I want to shine Your light for all to see—the light of evangelism and the light of soulful rest. Show me how to be the best witness I can for You! Amen.

Grab the Promised Hope

We who have run for our very lives to God have every reason to grab the promised hope with both hands and never let go. It's an unbreakable spiritual lifeline, reaching past all appearances right to the very presence of God where Jesus, running on ahead of us, has taken up his permanent post as high priest for us, in the order of Melchizedek.

HEBREWS 6:18–20 MSG

Sometimes we toil because we don't trust God. We slave away, killing ourselves, destroying our health, because we simply don't have faith that the Lord will take care of us. In our minds, we draw up a blueprint for fixing a particular situation, and then we work that plan. But in the process of doing so, we almost work ourselves into an early grave.

God will take care of you. Read those words again: *God will take care of you*. Sure, you have your part to do—but don't add stress worrying over how, when, or where He'll come through. Just rest in the knowledge that He *will*. You have this promise from His Word!

Jesus, your great high priest, has gone ahead of you. He has made provision for literally everything. Knowing you have an advocate like that should bring great peace!

Lord, remind me that I need to trust You with every aspect of my life, including my daily provision. My soul can rest when I place my trust in You. Today I choose to do just that! Amen.

Rest in His Presence

And he said, "My presence will go with you, and I will give you rest."
Exodus 33:14 ESV

When Moses and the Israelites trekked across the desert toward the Promised Land, God's presence led the way. Can you imagine countless thousands of people traveling together toward a common destination? (Ever tried to corral a few family members at an amusement park?) But when it came to Moses and the Israelites, God's own presence was the driving force. And when He leads the way, anything is possible.

Even rest.

Think about that. The Israelites were traveling on foot. . .in a hot desert. . .to an unknown destination. They were probably exhausted before they got a few miles into the trip—and that journey ultimately lasted forty years! Talk about wiped out. It's interesting, then, that God specifically promised the people *rest*.

He's promised us the same thing. Even in the midst of the journey. Even in the midst of the pain. Even in the midst of the chaos and confusion. Even there, He promises rest. You can step away—if not physically, at least mentally and spiritually—and garner the rest you need to keep going.

You *can* keep going. But first. . .rest.

Lord, I thank You for the promise of rest!
Even now, I'll depend on You to give it. Amen.

Fullness of Joy

You make known to me the path of life; in your presence there is fullness of joy; at your right hand are pleasures forevermore.
Psalm 16:11 ESV

There's just something about being in God's presence that makes life seem right again. When political upheaval swirls around you, hide away in His presence. When thorny situations at work threaten to rob you of your peace, run to His side. When that person who always grates on your nerves (you know the one) starts in. . .take off running, girl. Go straight to the Savior. He's been there all along, just waiting for your arrival.

If you knew you could trade tension for peace, would you? If you realized you could swap frustration for fullness of joy, would that be worth it? Great rest can be found in your time with the Savior, so don't put it off any longer. *He is the answer*. He's always been the answer. Run to Him today to turn your rough situations around. In His presence is fullness of joy.

I won't wait, Jesus. I'll come running straight into Your arms. There I will find rest for my weary soul. There I will be at peace. And there I will experience pleasures forevermore. What more could a girl want? Thank You, Lord. Amen.

The Cool of the Day

And they heard the sound of the Lord God walking in the garden in the cool of the day, and the man and his wife hid themselves from the presence of the Lord God among the trees of the garden.
Genesis 3:8 ESV

What a fascinating verse from the Bible's first book. Adam and Eve were hiding, hoping the Lord wouldn't figure out what they'd done. (As if!) After munching that forbidden fruit, they'd gained a completely different perspective on things. Suddenly, they knew life was about to change. . .big-time!

God knew what they had done, of course, and loved them in spite of it. But He also needed to conduct a little business with them. That's where our story picks up.

The Creator of all things was taking a quiet stroll in a garden. Can you even picture that? He chose that particular time of day, the coolest part of the day, for a quiet walk. Maybe He was gearing up for the big task ahead—namely, confronting His kids.

Might there be a lesson here for us? No matter what you're facing, it's going to be easier after you've taken the time to calm your heart, your mind, and your spirit.

So take a quiet stroll, girl. Cool down. Then face your issue head-on.

Lord, I'll simmer down and take a little stroll to get Your perspective! Amen.

Come Close to God

Come near to God and he will come near to you. Wash your hands, you sinners, and purify your hearts, you double-minded.
JAMES 4:8 NIV

Back in the '70s, there was a commercial for a particular hair product. A woman and man were running toward each other in a field, getting closer, closer, closer. Finally, the announcer spoke: "The closer she gets, the better she looks!"

Hardly politically correct, but here's a fun spiritual slant: The closer you get to God, the better *He* looks. His heart is revealed in the closeness.

Now look again at today's scripture. It's a promise. If you draw near to God, He will draw near to you. It's a call to action, friend, not a suggestion. The closer you get, the closer He gets.

"How do I do that?" you might ask. The answer is found in the rest of the verse. Get your heart and mind ready. Prepare yourself for an encounter. Get rid of doubt by reminding yourself of the promises He's made in His Word and already fulfilled in your life. Then it's as simple as taking steps in His direction!

I'm drawing close today, Lord! I see Your beauty. I see Your glory. I feel Your heart beating, and I'm grateful because I know You love me. Amen.

To Dwell with Him

One thing I ask from the LORD, this only do I seek: that I may dwell in the house of the LORD all the days of my life, to gaze on the beauty of the LORD and to seek him in his temple.

PSALM 27:4 NIV

Norah married a man who made her life very difficult. He had some personal struggles—alcohol abuse being at the top of the list. On good days, the man could be very demanding and rude. Life became almost intolerable until he finally gave his problem to the Lord, once and for all.

During their tumultuous years, though, Norah felt trapped. She hated the way she felt in her own home—unsafe, insecure, unstable. She couldn't settle her spirit and be at rest. No way. . .not until this problem was solved.

Maybe you've been there. Something about your environment has made you feel trapped. You've been looking for a way out.

God may work a miracle and provide a resolution like Norah's. Or He might not. One thing is certain: You never have to feel stuck as far as your relationship with Jesus is concerned. You'll never be looking for a trap door. You won't be running for the hills. With Him you're safer than you've ever been. . .and you can rest easy.

I can safely dwell with You, my precious Savior. How grateful I am. My soul is at rest. Amen.

In Peace I Will Lie Down

In peace I will both lie down and sleep; for you alone, O Lord, make me dwell in safety.
Psalm 4:8 ESV

Have you heard that old adage, "Don't go to sleep angry"? It's a biblical principle, actually, found in the book of Ephesians: "'Don't sin by letting anger control you.' Don't let the sun go down while you are still angry" (Ephesians 4:26 NLT).

Why do you suppose God cares about your frame of mind when you go to bed at night? Well, He wants you to lie down in peace, to rest your head on the pillow without ten thousand errant thoughts keeping you awake.

Those icky nights when you toss and turn? Yeah, they're no fun. So God—as always—has a better plan: Take care of business before you turn in.

Some folks say, "Don't go to bed angry—stay awake and fight it out!" Maybe that's better than tossing and turning all night, eaten up with frustration and worry. But why do either when God is ready and willing to give you peace?

I want a good night's sleep, Lord. So I'll get things figured out before I put my head on the pillow. Help me to process and deal with the hard things so peaceful sleep follows. Amen.

Sleep in Heavenly Peace

If you lie down, you will not be afraid;
when you lie down, your sleep will be sweet.
Proverbs 3:24 ESV

"Sleep in heavenly peace." Those aren't just lyrics to a familiar Christmas carol; they're God's desire for you every single night. He doesn't want you to toss and turn, to be so riddled with anxiety that you can't doze off. Instead, He longs for you to trust Him so deeply, so intimately, that you don't have a care in the world as your head hits the pillow.

We were probably too young to remember it clearly, but our mothers likely sang lullabies to us when we were babies. At least we've seen other moms do that. Cradled in the arms of her mother, a baby is wooed to sleep by a gentle song. She's distracted from teething pain or tummy ache, lulled to peaceful rest by Mama's melody.

God Himself is the perfect parent. And He's right there, singing His song over *you*. He wants to calm your spirit so you really can sleep in heavenly peace. Just stop. Listen. Rest.

I hear Your melody, even now, Lord! Thank You for singing over me and calming my troubled heart. Amen.

The Sleep of a Laborer

Sweet is the sleep of a laborer, whether he eats little or much,
but the full stomach of the rich will not let him sleep.
ECCLESIASTES 5:12 ESV

Years ago, the Beatles came out with a song called "Hard Day's Night." When you've spent all day working—whether you're mucking stalls or hunched over a computer for hours—you're wiped out. And when you're exhausted, nothing feels as good as your bed.

Back in Bible days they didn't have high-end mattresses and box springs. There were no special pillows molded to fit your neck. Cooling sheets or electric blankets? Nope. Beds back then were pretty primitive. But you don't hear David or Peter or Paul grumbling about their sleep status. None of them took the time to compose a verse about how uncomfortable they were at night. Most likely, once they lay down, they went out like lights. Their hard work led to an excellent night's sleep.

You need that too, girl. You work hard—whether you're at home all day with the kids or wrestling clients or customers in the marketplace. Don't add unnecessary stress in the evening—take a bubble bath, read a good book, or listen to relaxing music (maybe all three), then tumble into bed for a good night's sleep!

I need rest, Jesus. I'm grateful for my bed—
and a hot shower or bubble bath too. Thanks for
modern-day luxuries so that I can rest better. Amen.

Rested, Tall, and Steady

I stretch myself out. I sleep. Then I'm up again—rested, tall and steady, fearless before the enemy mobs coming at me from all sides.
PSALM 3:5–6 MSG

When you know the enemy is coming hard and fast on your heels, you run like the dickens! The last thing on your mind is settling down for a good night's sleep. A battlefield is no place for rest. Unless your commander is Jesus.

Make no mistake—this life is a battlefield. But here's the cool thing about walking with Jesus: You can sleep peacefully, no matter how many enemies come after you. Financial woes? Sleep tight. Relational issues? *Zzzzz.* Job problems? Give them over to God and rest peacefully, knowing that the Lord is your defender. He's your rock, your fortress, your defense.

Go ahead—stretch out on that bed. Grab your favorite pillow and cuddle up. Let those eyes flutter closed. When you awaken you'll be rested, tall, and steady, ready for whatever comes your way.

When God is on your side, you can be fearless before the enemy. Just ask little David, who stood up to Goliath. He would have a "tall" tale to tell!

I'll be ready for the tasks ahead when I'm rested, Lord. Thanks for the reminder that I can be fearless. But first. . .sleep! Amen.

Sleep in Trust

Hurry with your answer, God! I'm nearly at the end of my rope. Don't turn away; don't ignore me! That would be certain death. If you wake me each morning with the sound of your loving voice, I'll go to sleep each night trusting in you. Point out the road I must travel; I'm all ears, all eyes before you. Save me from my enemies, God—you're my only hope! Teach me how to live to please you, because you're my God. Lead me by your blessed Spirit into cleared and level pastureland.

Psalm 143:7–10 msg

Have you ever reached the end of your rope? Maybe you're there now. Evie knew that feeling well. After years of a tough relationship with her grown daughter, things came to a head. Madison's addiction to prescription pain pills was wrecking both of their lives.

Or so Evie thought.

After some time to herself, she came to a revelation—she wasn't put on this planet to fix her grown daughter's problem. Evie could pray for Madison, but the time had come to keep a healthy distance. Once she realized this and implemented a plan to step away, her life calmed down. She was finally able to sleep at night, trusting that God could—even without her help!—take care of the situation. He can, you know.

Some situations are so big that only God can fix them. Will you let Him?

I get it, Lord! I can only sleep in trust when I hand the reins over to You. I choose to do that today. Amen.

Be Still and Know

"Be still, and know that I am God. I will be exalted among the nations, I will be exalted in the earth!"
PSALM 46:10 ESV

"How do you know?"

"Know what?" Meredith looked into her daughter's anxious eyes.

"Anything. How do you know anything? Like what job to take, who to marry, what to do? How do you know. . .for sure?"

"Oh." Meredith chuckled. "Well, it's a matter of hearing from God, and the only way to truly hear from Him is to be still and listen."

"Be still and listen," Lyn repeated, then sighed. "There's my problem. I'm so busy it's hard to be still and listen to anyone, let alone God."

Maybe you can relate. You're struggling to know what to do in a particular situation. You can't quite figure it out. You wish God would speak in an audible voice and just tell you.

Here's the truth, friend: He *is* speaking. He's whispering in that still, small voice, hoping you'll step away from the madness, still your heart, and hear Him.

It takes shutting out all the other voices in order to hear His. What noise do you need to cancel today? Rest in God, listening only for His still, small voice.

Lord, the voices around me can be so loud.
I want to step away so I can hear You more clearly.
Shout if You need to, Jesus—I'm listening. Amen.

Slow Down, Girl!

Be still before the LORD and wait patiently for him;
fret not yourself over the one who prospers in his way,
over the man who carries out evil devices!
PSALM 37:7 ESV

When you're still—really still—you have the ability to hear, see, and believe with more intensity. Busyness can be a huge distraction, for sure. And busyness can lead to a serious lack of trust in God. Why? When you're moving too fast, you can forget that the enemy of your soul is just bluffing with his lies. You can start to believe them when everything around you is in flux.

Today, be reminded that the devil is powerless against the almighty God. Satan arrives when things are swirling around you because he knows that's when you're vulnerable. Distracted. Down. Then he tries to take you out.

But that won't happen since God is on your side. So slow down. Take a breath. Calm your heart. Then lean in close and listen to the only voice that matters. God's got a lot to say to you, even when you're under attack. *Especially* then.

I see how the enemy comes after me, Jesus, but I'm onto him! I won't let him knock me down. I'll lean in and listen only to You. Amen.

God Will Fight for You

"The LORD *will fight for you, and all you have to do is keep still."*
EXODUS 14:14 GNT

Julianna was a fixer. As soon as she heard that a loved one was facing a problem, she would sweep in to fix it. A sick friend in need of medicine? She'd be at the pharmacy in a flash. A family member low on groceries? Five bags were on their way. But when she tried to intervene in her daughter's marital woes, things got out of hand.

Maybe you can relate. We all have a bit of Julianna in us. We think we have the ability (and responsibility) to tackle anything—even battles that aren't ours to fight. This desire to fix things can land us in the hot seat, in the middle of some very awkward and uncomfortable situations. Then we squirm, trying to decide how to get out of the mess. . .the mess we were never supposed to be part of in the first place.

God is the fixer. He's the one to fight the battles. Sure, it's good and right to care for those in need—don't stop that. But use your spiritual antennae to know when enough is enough. Stay close to God in Bible study and prayer, and ask the Spirit to show you the line in the sand. Once He does, don't tiptoe over it! You keep still. God will fight the battle.

Please rid me of my fix-it tendencies, Lord! I hand the reins to You so that I can have peace and rest in my soul. Amen.

Stand Firm and See

"You will not have to fight this battle. Take up your positions; stand firm and see the deliverance the LORD will give you, Judah and Jerusalem. Do not be afraid; do not be discouraged. Go out to face them tomorrow, and the LORD will be with you."

2 CHRONICLES 20:17 NIV

This world often puts Christians in a hard spot. Have you ever come out swinging on some important issue, then later folded like a lawn chair? It's hard to stand tall, especially when others around you bow down. We fickle human beings think we're strong, but when the pressure comes it's easy to give in.

Maybe you've been standing firm, holding out faithfully for some big thing from God. The battle can be intense and wearying. You don't know how much longer you can hold up.

Think about Moses, leading the Israelites toward the Promised Land. When the enemy rose up to fight, he climbed a nearby hill to hold his hands over the battlefield. As long as those arms were raised, the Israelites prevailed. When he got weary and dropped his hands, the enemy advanced. Just a little pressure there, huh?

Moses needed the help of two good friends who held up his arms for him. We can lean on trusted friends too, but know that the ultimate victory comes from God alone. Stand firm, girl. You will see the deliverance of the Lord if you don't give up.

I won't quit, Lord. I want to finish well and then enjoy the rest You've promised. Help me stand strong, I pray. Amen.

Quiet Down in There!

Quiet down before God, be prayerful before him. Don't bother with those who climb the ladder, who elbow their way to the top.
PSALM 37:7 MSG

"Quiet down in there!" Maybe you heard those words as a kid. Or maybe you've spoken them as an adult. When things get loud, we tell the annoying ones to "quiet down."

Why not try that in your spiritual life? When Satan comes in like an out-of-tune brass band, you can say, "Quiet down, you!" That's when God's Spirit can sweep in to help calm your soul.

Quiet is so important. In the craziness of life, have you ever said, "I can't think straight!"? And that's what the enemy of your soul counts on. He wants to disrupt your ability to concentrate. He's hoping to throw you off course.

But no matter how loud the voices get, peace is possible. It's not up to you, at least not entirely. Your role is simply to look the enemy in the eye and whisper, "Hey, you. . .shush!" Add the words "in the name of Jesus," and he has to flee!

I'm so grateful for the quiet moments, Lord. Speak in such a way that I hear and understand. Drown out the other voices, I pray. May I keep my focus always and only on You! Amen.

Anxious for Nothing

Do not be anxious about anything, but in everything by prayer and supplication with thanksgiving let your requests be made known to God. And the peace of God, which surpasses all understanding, will guard your hearts and your minds in Christ Jesus.

Philippians 4:6–7 ESV

Don't be anxious about anything.

Read that again.

Anything means, well, *anything*.

Think of the last time you were really wound up about something. What triggered the anxiety? Did it tie your stomach in knots? Jumble your thoughts? How did you respond? What if you had just decided, "I'm not going to be anxious about stuff like that anymore"?

Deciding to lay down anxiety is half the battle. Once we realize we have that kind of power, the rest is a breeze. Think of it like this: Anxiety is like a hot pan on the stove. You can reach to grab it. . .or not. If you do, you know you're going to get burned. If you don't, you won't.

So stop grabbing the pan. Let God take it. He's the only one who can fix your situation anyway, right? Your job is to trust Him. Let Him know what you're thinking. Let Him know what You're feeling. Then trust Him to take care of things. *Anything*.

I want to stop grabbing the pan, Jesus! May I be anxious. . .for nothing! I'll place my concerns in Your hands and trust You to handle them. Amen.

Not as the World Gives

"Peace I leave with you; my peace I give you. I do not give to you as the world gives. Do not let your hearts be troubled and do not be afraid."
JOHN 14:27 NIV

Don't let your heart be troubled.

Emma read those words over and over, but they didn't seem to sink in. With her house in disrepair, the kids sick with the flu, and her husband facing a possible job loss, she couldn't seem to do anything but fret. This whole idea of peace in the middle of chaos was foreign to her, though she wanted to give it a try. You can only go so long with your heart twisted in knots, after all.

Maybe you can relate. The situation is so dire, the problems so big that they seem impossible.

Here's the truth: The only fixer is God Himself. Oh, you can go get a massage, or see a therapist, or drink some chamomile tea. The world has some legitimately helpful things, but they are temporary at best. The massage will wear off. The therapy never really seems to be done. That tea? Well, the bag only lasts so long.

God's peace, though? It lasts forever. It never weakens. So trust Him, even when life feels impossible. He can bring rest to your soul if you'll just let Him.

Lord, I don't want to be tangled up inside. I don't want to look for answers on my own. I know that only You can fix what I'm going through, so I give these situations to You. Amen.

The Prodigal Returns

God met me more than halfway, he freed me from my anxious fears.
Psalm 34:4 MSG

"God met me more than halfway." Isn't that a lovely notion?

Think about the prodigal son, returning home after squandering his inheritance. As he appeared on the road to his home, his father came running. That's how your heavenly Father is! He sees you coming, and before you can say, "Dad, I blew it," He's already got you wrapped in His arms, offering forgiveness.

Do you need to turn back toward home today? Have you wandered too far away? Like the prodigal son, you will never find rest for your soul until you finally go back where you belong—to the arms of the Father. Once you're there, all the burdens that have been weighing you down will fade away in the light of His glory and grace.

Oh, what a wonderful Father. Oh, what a wonderful friend! He's running down the road, even now, arms outstretched!

Lord, thank You for meeting me halfway. I'm sorry I wandered away in the first place. I've learned a lot—like what not to do. But You've been gracious and kind, and now I'm finally at rest, safe in Your arms. Thank You for welcoming me back home. Amen.

Add an Hour?

"And which of you by being anxious can
add a single hour to his span of life?"
MATTHEW 6:27 ESV

Every day people work to lengthen their lives. They join gyms. They go on diets. They visit doctors. And all with one goal in mind: to live longer. For some, it's working. Many people these days live into their nineties and even past a hundred.

Really, though, we don't control the number of our days. Face it: You could work yourself into the best shape of your life and get hit by a bus while crossing the street. Hey, things like that happen.

Here's the point: God knows the number of our days, as well as the way those days will play out. He's also aware of a key truth that we as Christians often forget—we are already on the road to eternity. So when our lives end here on earth, they simply continue in His presence in heaven.

You can't add to the *number* of your days, but you can add to their *value*. Every moment spent with God—every moment you follow hard after Jesus—will be one less moment you'll spend in anxiety.

Rest easy. Give your days, no matter how many you might have, to the Lord.

I won't fret over the number of days in my life, Jesus.
Instead, I'll fill them with precious moments spent with You. Amen.

Be Strong and Courageous!

"Haven't I commanded you? Strength! Courage! Don't be timid; don't get discouraged. God, your God, is with you every step you take."
Joshua 1:9 MSG

What does courage have to do with rest? Everything. Throughout His Word, God has urged us to be strong and courageous. If He felt strongly enough to repeat such commands, we'd better sit up and pay attention, right?

He told Joshua, "Don't be timid; don't get discouraged. God, your God, is with you every step you take." In other words, He's got us covered. Knowing that should put our minds at ease.

Think about this: Courage begets courage. The stronger you are today, the stronger you'll be tomorrow. And the time in between? Those hours your head is on the pillow? You'll be able to get the rest you need because you're not knotted up in fear.

So square those shoulders! If little David could face his giant problems head-on, you can too. Courage isn't just a good idea God thought up. . .it's His will for your life!

I want to be courageous, Lord, but I can't do it on my own. I need Your fortitude, Your strength, and Your supernatural power. Help me, I pray. Amen.

Sabbath Rest

And on the seventh day God finished his work that he had done, and he rested on the seventh day from all his work that he had done. So God blessed the seventh day and made it holy, because on it God rested from all his work that he had done in creation.

GENESIS 2:2–3 ESV

God took a day off! What does that tell you? If the all-powerful Lord—who has the kind of energy it takes to create worlds—chose to rest, you most certainly should too.

There are a couple of key words in this verse. When did God rest? *After* of the work He had done in creation. Also, consider that the Lord *blessed* this special day. Our own day of rest, which God commanded, is blessed too.

So what keeps you from enjoying a Sabbath rest? Are you a girl who has a hard time taking a break? Maybe you say, "I know I should rest, but I might just tidy up around the house today." Or, "I know I should stay home, but my boss asked me to get in some extra hours and I hate to tell him no."

Some days you really just need to kick your feet up, resting your body, mind, and heart. If you don't take a Sabbath rest, those other six days are going to be pretty overwhelming. You know it's true.

Lord, thank You for the Sabbath. I'll do my best to enter into Your rest on this blessed and holy day. "Because" of the other six, I'll rest on the seventh. . .and be "blessed." Amen.

Rest, a Holy Act

Then God blessed the seventh day and made it holy, because on it he rested from all the work of creating that he had done.
GENESIS 2:3 NIV

Have you ever considered rest a holy act? God does. When He consecrated the Sabbath, He "blessed" that special day and "made it holy."

So what does a holy rest day look like in the twenty-first century? It might mean saying no to some fun activities. It might require you to take a serious look at your schedule—and slow down. It might even mean a little getaway from those you love most, simply to refresh your heart and mind.

Becki believed in rest as a holy act. She decided to dedicate one day a week as a time of rest before God. She said no to distractions, hunkering down to give her heart, mind, and body time to recoup from the week prior—and prep for the week ahead. As a result, she felt rested, invigorated, and stronger.

God wants His girls to be as strong as they can be. And that can only happen when you take the time to rest.

*Lord, I'll set aside a special holy time with You.
Thank You for the reminder. Amen.*

Rest Remains

There remains, then, a Sabbath-rest for the people of God; for anyone who enters God's rest also rests from their works, just as God did from his.
HEBREWS 4:9–10 NIV

Many people would argue that we no longer need a Sabbath rest because we're not under the old law. There's some truth to that argument, but consider today's scripture, from the New Testament: "There *remains*, then, a Sabbath-rest." These words were penned long after Jesus' death on the cross ushered in the new covenant. Still, the writer of Hebrews was led by God's Spirit to use the word *remains*.

It's not a legalistic thing. The Sabbath is no longer a day of dos and don'ts. It's simply a gift from God for His people—a day set aside to chill. To be with our Lord. To reenergize. To refresh.

Check out verse 10 for the rest of the story. (Get it? The "rest" of the story?) *You can enter God's rest*. Open the door and walk right through. So when you're taking that day off, don't spend it in front of a screen. Enter into God's presence! That's His desire in the first place, that you spend more time with Him.

Lord, I'll enter in. I won't put it off. I'm so grateful a Sabbath-rest remains so that I can be refreshed in You. Amen.

A Song for the Sabbath

A psalm. A song. For the Sabbath day. It is good to praise the LORD and make music to your name, O Most High.
PSALM 92:1 NIV

Don't you love that this psalm is labeled "a song for the Sabbath day"? That's how it is when you're feeling refreshed. You're more likely to sing a song of praise, to have the energy to worship. When you're wiped out, down in the dumps, and feeling overwhelmed, praise doesn't come as naturally.

Benita learned this the hard way. After a particularly tough work week, she forced herself to go to church. With zero downtime, she hadn't properly rested in days. And when it came time to worship—usually one of her favorite things—she just couldn't. She sat in the pew, frozen in place, so tired she couldn't even stand.

That's what happens when we don't take care of ourselves. We pay a price physically, yes—but there's also a spiritual toll. It's hard to stay on top of any aspect of life when we're wiped out.

So get the rest you need. Take a Sabbath break. Then watch as God restores your Sabbath song!

I love it, Lord. I want to lift my voice in praise to You. Give me the rest I need so that I can sing with my whole heart. Amen.

Carrying a Load

This is what the LORD says: Be careful not to carry a load on the Sabbath day or bring it through the gates of Jerusalem.
JEREMIAH 17:21 NIV

What an interesting verse is Jeremiah 17:21! Of the many Old Testament rules related to the Sabbath, we see here that God's people were not allowed to "carry a load" on the Sabbath.

That'll preach, won't it? Even today, when we're free from the demands of the old law, we can see the benefit of not "carrying a load" while we try to rest our hearts, minds, and spirits. When you're burdened with the cares of life, trying to lift loads that were never yours to carry in the first place, it's hard to enjoy that Sabbath rest.

And yet, we do. We pick up unnecessary burdens then wonder why we're exhausted, zapped of strength. We wonder why we can't sleep at night, why we toss and turn.

What load are you carrying today? Aren't you ready to drop it? It's time. God wants you to relinquish that burden to Him so you can be set free. He's strong enough to carry whatever it is that weighs you down. He always has been and always will be.

I'm dropping this load so that I can enjoy my Sabbath rest, Lord! I'm so weary with dragging this around. I give it to You today. Amen.

Walk in His Way

Thus says the LORD: "Stand by the roads, and look, and ask for the ancient paths, where the good way is; and walk in it, and find rest for your souls. But they said, 'We will not walk in it.'"
JEREMIAH 6:16 ESV

Imagine you're in the woods. There's a clearly marked path in front of you, but you decide to take off down a tiny trail to your right. Just a few steps in, you're starting to question your decision. As the trail diminishes and you're surrounded by undergrowth, you're really nervous. Should you turn around? Can you even find your way back now?

Yes, that's a picture of our way through life.

Here's the thing: God has laid out a perfect map for us. It's called the Bible, and the pathway it describes is perfect. Scripture will lead you straight to your desired destination. It will give you advice on living a safe, contented, worthy life.

But most of us are prone to wander. So we occasionally take off down those proverbial bunny trails, convinced we've got a better way.

Only it's not. Our own paths lead to chaos, confusion, and fear. If you stick to the "ancient paths"—the way, the truth, and the life—you won't go wrong. Find the Lord's path. Walk in it. Find rest for your soul. It's really that easy.

I get it, Jesus. I have found Your path, but I have to stay on it. I don't want to be stubborn or prideful, insisting on my own way. Please keep my feet from wandering. Amen.

Walk Humbly with Your God

He has shown you, O mortal, what is good. And what does the LORD require of you? To act justly and to love mercy and to walk humbly with your God.

MICAH 6:8 NIV

God has shown you what to do. His Word is filled with practical guidance to lead you every step of the way. The problem is you're human. You don't always follow the instructions. (It's true. . . remember that time you tried to assemble that bookshelf or bake that cake without following the instructions? How well did that work out?)

Instructions are there for a reason. And the Bible is the best guide ever. So it's a good idea—no, make that "an absolutely essential idea"—to follow its advice. The Lord used hundreds of years and dozens of writers to send you that message. It's probably worth your time!

Besides studying His Word, what else does God expect of you? To act justly (that is, treat people fairly), to love mercy (His to you and your own to others), and to walk humbly with Him (don't be a show-off or pretend to have your act together). When you live like this—when you love like this—you exemplify Christ to a lost and dying world. And guess what? This kind of life is filled with peace, joy, and rest. It's a win-win!

I will walk humbly with You, God. You've shown me what to do. Please help me do it! Amen.

Walk with God

"True instruction was in his mouth and nothing false was found on his lips. He walked with me in peace and uprightness, and turned many from sin."
MALACHI 2:6 NIV

Take a young puppy out for a walk and you'll quickly learn how difficult that process can be. He strains and charges ahead. He chases every squirrel. He sniffs every blade of grass. In short, he couldn't care less about the person holding his leash. He's completely distracted by what's in front of him.

Sometimes we're like that with God. He has a firm grip on us, but we're off chasing squirrels. Or job opportunities. Or relationships. Or that next big thrill. We're sniffing blades of grass. Or partying with friends. Or tugging, tugging, tugging against His hand, determined we know a better way.

But we don't. He's called *Lord* for a reason. He truly knows best. He guides best. He loves best. And when we surrender to Him, when we stop fighting and simply walk alongside as He charts our course, we can rest easy. We can be at peace.

Stop tugging at the leash, girl. Really.

Lord, I'm sorry I keep pulling away. I'm easily distracted. Please set my eyes on You and help me surrender to Your leading. Amen.

Let's Meet Up!

"Do two walk together, unless they have agreed to meet?"
AMOS 3:3 ESV

Maggie sat in the restaurant, staring at her phone. The minutes ticked by. Why wasn't Katie there yet? Weren't they supposed to meet for dinner at six o'clock?

When 6:30 rolled around, Maggie gave up on her friend. She went ahead and ordered dinner. As she ate alone, aggravation set in. Why did Katie stand her up?

Turned out, Katie hadn't. As Maggie scrolled back up through her texts, she noticed one she'd overlooked—the one in which Katie explained that she wasn't feeling well and would have to postpone dinner. *Oops*.

These things happen. But it's always disappointing when you think you're going to connect with someone and it doesn't happen.

So imagine how God must feel. We say, "I'll chat with You tomorrow, Lord," or "I'll get into the Bible on January 1, I promise." Then we forget. We make other plans. We don't feel well.

Walking with God—which is what brings peace and rest to our lives—requires sacrifice. It takes relationship. God is sending you an invitation to dine, not just for one meal, but every day. Don't stand Him up!

I won't stand You up, Lord! I'm looking forward to our time together. Amen.

Return for Healing

"This people's heart has grown dull, and with their ears they can barely hear, and their eyes they have closed, lest they should see with their eyes and hear with their ears and understand with their heart and turn, and I would heal them."

MATTHEW 13:15 ESV

Sometimes we wonder why healing doesn't come. Why our hearts are still broken. Why our thoughts are still troubled. Why we're still dealing with chronic issues. Some of these trials drag on for years, and we despair of finding relief.

Some of our physical and spiritual struggles are entwined with psychological issues. An ongoing stomach issue can be tied to a case of nerves—perhaps you're anxious and worked up because you're angry with another person. Or maybe you have chronic migraines because you're in a job situation you should have left years ago. These things happen.

The answer to these struggles is always the same: Return to God. Return for healing of heart. Return for healing of mind. Return for healing of body. Return so that your spirit can be made whole, your soul can be at rest. And return so that He can guide you to the place you're really supposed to be.

I'm coming back to You, Jesus. All of my answers are found in You. When I run into Your arms, my heartbreak is mended, my troubled thoughts are made whole. I'm done with doing things my way! Amen.

In Returning You Will Be Saved

For thus said the Lord God, the Holy One of Israel,
"In returning and rest you shall be saved; in quietness and in trust shall be your strength." But you were unwilling.
Isaiah 30:15 ESV

Think of a naughty toddler on the run from his mama. She's calling out to him, but he deliberately turns in the opposite direction with a firm "No!" on his lips. He runs from her safety, her protection, her arms. . .but never her love. When he finally relents, there's usually some pain involved.

It's the same way when we run from God, isn't it? We lift a defiant fist with a "No!" on our lips, then take off ready to do our own thing, to go our own way. In the end, we're worn out, chastened, and ready to admit, "I should've just done it *His* way."

How often we try to force life to work according to our desires. That's like trying to jam puzzle pieces into the wrong spot. The picture will never be perfect until you do things the right way.

Stick with God. Don't run. Don't hide. In the end, heading to His arms will give you the rest and peace you need.

I'm done with running, Jesus! No more defiant nos from me!
If I run, it will be straight into Your arms to find rest. Amen.

No Cherry-Picking!

All Scripture is inspired by God and is useful for teaching, for showing people what is wrong in their lives, for correcting faults, and for teaching how to live right.
2 TIMOTHY 3:16 NCV

Some people love to cherry-pick their verses from scripture, choosing only the peppy, chipper ones. They sail right over the harder stuff, convinced a more positive approach is best.

But life is hard. And those tough verses? They're there for a reason. Sure, you don't want to overload on negativity, but sometimes you need to be reminded that the great men and women of old struggled too. They had problems that stopped them cold. And yet, miraculously, they went on to do great things for God.

You're doing great things for Him too. Yes, you've had bumps in the road. And yes, you've made a few mistakes. But you're growing, you're learning, and you have a good head on your shoulders. You'll move forward from here, stronger and braver.

Don't fight the seasons, sister! Learn from them instead.

I won't fight, Lord. I know that even the great men and women of the Bible had bad days. I'll take the bad with the good and learn from it all, with Your help. Amen.

Rend Your Heart

Rend your heart and not your garments. Return to the LORD your God, for he is gracious and compassionate, slow to anger and abounding in love, and he relents from sending calamity.

JOEL 2:13 NIV

Back in biblical days, people would demonstrate strong emotion by rending (tearing) their clothes. This was an outward show of the grief inside. In today's scripture we see an admonition to rend your *heart*, not your garments. Interesting—but what does that mean?

When you rend your heart, you're opening it up so that God can take control. In one sense, to rend means you're giving up. But in another sense, you're giving *over*. Over to God. Over to the hands that created you. Over to the one who can handle your issue, whatever it may be.

When you give your heart to the King of all kings, when you return to Him, He treats you graciously. Compassionately. He's not waiting with rod in hand, ready to give you a thrashing. He's just thrilled that you're with Him.

What's troubling you today? Is God calling you to rend your heart so that healing can come?

Lord, today I rend my heart. I rip it wide open and give it as an offering to You. Take it, Jesus, and bring healing, I pray. Amen.

Wholehearted

"I will make them want to know me, that I am the LORD.
They will be my people, and I will be their God,
because they will return to me with their whole hearts."
JEREMIAH 24:7 NCV

Have you ever done something half-heartedly? Maybe you had to clean the house but didn't feel like it. Or it was time to pay the mortgage and you thought you'd rather not. Those half-hearted efforts clearly don't carry the same excitement as a full-on, zeal-filled response.

Oh, but God wants His wandering kids to return to Him enthusiastically. He doesn't want you to come back with your tail between your legs. None of that! God wants to see a broad smile on your face and hear a "Great to be back!" on your lips.

In short, He wants you to return home trusting that He will welcome you with open arms. God will, you know, no matter what you've done. No matter where you've been. No matter who you've been with. You can run eagerly into His arms today to find the rest and peace you've been longing for.

Lord, I'll be enthusiastic in my response to You!
No half-hearted efforts on my part. I'm coming,
fully engaged and ready to give my whole heart. Amen.

Lay Aside Every Weight

Therefore, since we are surrounded by so great a cloud of witnesses, let us also lay aside every weight, and sin which clings so closely, and let us run with endurance the race that is set before us.

HEBREWS 12:1 ESV

We carry a lot of weights. Oh, not the physical kind. We carry the weight of sin. The weight of pain. The weight of grief. The weight of a broken heart. And, after time, those weights can become too much to bear. We find ourselves in a never-ending struggle, feeling literally weighed down by it all. We want to be free but don't know where to begin.

Good news: Jesus is the weight bearer. When He went to the cross, agonizing in physical and spiritual pain, He demonstrated His willingness to carry the weight of the world on His shoulders. And in His heart. His love appeared on His hands and feet and in His side.

Jesus carried it all. It's already been done. So those weights *you're* dragging around? They are no longer yours to carry. Place them in Jesus' hands once and for all and be free. Your heart, soul, and mind can be at rest!

You did it all, Jesus. There's nothing left for me to do but place it all in Your hands! Today I choose to do just that so that I can finally rest easy in You. Amen.

An Invitation to the Ball

"Come to me, all who labor and are heavy laden, and I will give you rest."
MATTHEW 11:28 ESV

Imagine you're Cinderella, receiving an invitation to the ball. Would you, for one second, consider not going? Of course not! You'd search for the ideal gown, fix your hair in the perfect style, and slip into the most beautiful shoes. Then you'd eagerly head out to the party.

God has sent *you* an invitation to the party of a lifetime—a ball where His Son is the guest of honor. And you are welcome, no matter what you look like or what you've done. Best of all, this party goes on and on and on. . .into eternity.

When God says, "Come," He offers you far more than a simple invitation. His "Come" means "*Come as you are.*" It means "Come with your guilt," "Come with your pain," "Come with your exhaustion."

And when you arrive, He takes those things that weigh you down, trading them for peace, joy, and hope.

Knowing that, why would you ever reject the invitation? Today the Lord says, "Come!" Run into His arms, Cinderella. What's keeping you?

I'm coming, Jesus! I won't make You wait any longer. Thank You for the invitation to spend eternity at the ball with You! Amen.

About God's Invitations

Come now, you who say, "Today or tomorrow we will go into such and such a town and spend a year there and trade and make a profit"—yet you do not know what tomorrow will bring. What is your life? For you are a mist that appears for a little time and then vanishes.

James 4:13–14 ESV

You've received an invitation to an important wedding. You can't wait! Nothing could stop you from attending.

Except something does. The day before the big event, you get sick. Now you're unable to attend this event you've been so eager to experience. You're devastated, but what can you do? You don't want to risk making other people sick on such a celebratory day.

Things like this happen. They are unexpected and outside our control. And they can wreck our emotions, causing stomach churn and loss of sleep.

Happily, nothing can interfere with the invitations God issues. No matter what your frame of mind, no matter what sickness or sin or struggle you're facing, you can show up. You never have to send a cancellation! Go to God, happy or not, sick or not, ready or not. You have an open invitation to spend eternity with Him.

What's stopping you? *Nothing*.

Lord, here I come! I accept Your invitation. I'm so grateful to be included. I'm Yours. . .forever! Amen.

Don't Sink!

Shortly before dawn Jesus went out to them, walking on the lake. When the disciples saw him walking on the lake, they were terrified. "It's a ghost," they said, and cried out in fear. But Jesus immediately said to them: "Take courage! It is I. Don't be afraid." "Lord, if it's you," Peter replied, "tell me to come to you on the water." "Come," he said.

MATTHEW 14:25–29 NIV

Imagine a toddler just learning to walk. She falls. . .a lot. But when she keeps her focus on Mom, she does a better job.

That's how it was that day on the Sea of Galilee when Peter made the impetuous (and monumental) decision to try to walk to Jesus. When he kept his eyes on the Savior, he stayed on top of the waves. The moment Peter got scared and looked away, he immediately sank.

You know that sinking feeling, don't you? We've all experienced it many times in our lives. When we thought we might lose the house. When we faced some terrible health crisis. When a loved one passed away. We felt sure we would go under.

But we didn't. Jesus reached out and saved us! Then, going forward, keeping our heads above water demanded that we focus on Him again, like we had at first. Fixing our eyes on Jesus will see us safely through any other storms we face.

Jesus will never let you down. He's kept you afloat before, and He'll do it again. Just keep your eyes on Him.

I'll stay focused on You, Jesus! Keep me from sinking, I pray. Amen.

No Other Way

Jesus said to him, "I am the way, and the truth, and the life. No one comes to the Father except through me."
JOHN 14:6 ESV

Many people are in turmoil because they don't know how to get to God. Many think they must work themselves there—if they do *x*, *y*, or *z*, they'll eventually reach heaven. Others claim to find God outside of Christ, but we know from scripture they're off course. These people never find their nirvana because they've left Jesus out of the equation. But the Bible makes it clear—there's no other way.

Let's examine Jesus' statement "I am the way, and the truth, and the life." He's the *only* way, the ultimate GPS. He's the *only* truth—no other "truth" out there will ultimately land you in heaven. And best of all, He's the life. . .the *only* life! No other religion leads to eternity with the one true God.

Now look at the rest of today's scripture: "No one comes to the Father except through me." Ouch. A lot of people don't like this part. They say, "Wait—I can't know God apart from Jesus?" The simple answer is "No." No Jesus, no God. But know Jesus, know God. He's the doorway that opens to the Father!

If you know Jesus, don't lose a minute's sleep over your future. Rest your soul in the loving shepherd who's never lost a single one of His sheep.

I'm coming through the only true door. . .Jesus!
Thank You, my Savior, for providing a way. Amen.

God Is Patient

The Lord is not slow in keeping his promise, as some understand slowness. Instead he is patient with you, not wanting anyone to perish, but everyone to come to repentance.
2 Peter 3:9 NIV

"The Lord is not slow in keeping his promise."

Jenna wasn't so sure about that. She told God on multiple occasions that she wanted to be married. She'd waited for years, but Mr. Right never came along. Now, well into her fifties, she was giving up. Jenna's disappointment was keen, as was her frustration toward God. Deep down, she somehow felt that He was to blame.

Patience isn't one of humanity's strong suits. We lose a lot of sleep over God's timetable. But think of how patient He's been with us! While we're chasing the things of this world, dabbling in sin or at least pushing the envelope—He's still at our side, loving us, gently wooing us home.

So don't give up. It's that simple and that hard. Don't give up on God, on His word, on your hopes and dreams, just because you haven't gotten your way yet.

God is good. He loves you. And He's very, very patient.

I get it, Lord! You've been patient with me. I need to be more patient—with You, with myself, and with others. Amen.

Wait on Him

For God alone my soul waits in silence;
from him comes my salvation.
PSALM 62:1 ESV

If you're like most people, you're not thrilled with waiting. You microwave your popcorn, text to communicate, and pay your bills online. You like things done lickety-split.

So, waiting on God? Ugh. But if you reread today's scripture, you'll find some helpful instruction: Have an expectant attitude while you wait on Him. "For God alone my soul waits," David wrote. Think about that. You're not waiting on a paycheck or a romantic relationship or even some miracle of healing. You're waiting on God Himself. That changes things, doesn't it?

Now add a small phrase to the line: Your soul is waiting *in silence*. You're not grumbling or complaining. Not whining and worrying. Not fussing or fighting. Your heart and mind are at rest, knowing God will come through for you—on His timetable. This discipline of intentionally honoring God in silence ultimately makes the waiting easier.

God knows you and your situation perfectly—and He has the wisdom and resources to take perfect care of you. Whatever you've dreamed up for yourself, His plan is ten thousand times better! So wait. He's going to come through for you.

I can trust You, Lord! I'll hang in there,
even though I don't know the outcome. Amen.

The Baby's Already Here!

We wait in hope for the LORD; he is our help and our shield.
PSALM 33:20 NIV

Ask an expectant mom, "What's the hardest thing about being pregnant?" You'll get a variety of answers. "Morning sickness" might make the list. Or "weight gain." "Pressure on the bladder" might be right up there. But with a moment's reflection, most would probably admit, "Waiting nine months to hold that baby in my arms."

When you know a baby is coming, you know a baby is coming. No one has to say, "Hey, I hope you have a baby one day!" You do have one. He or she is already here, just not in your arms.

That's how it is with the dreams God's given you. They're already here, even if they haven't yet come to fruition. You believe, way down deep, that God will fulfill His purpose in you. You know He'll come through, just as you expect a baby to be born.

You can rest easy in the waiting. No need to stress. No need to wonder. God's got you covered. Just wait.

I've never found it easy to wait, Lord, but I get it. I can totally trust You, even in the waiting. The baby's already here! Amen.

Don't Give Up

As she kept on praying to the Lord, Eli observed her mouth. Hannah was praying in her heart, and her lips were moving but her voice was not heard. Eli thought she was drunk and said to her, "How long are you going to stay drunk? Put away your wine."

1 Samuel 1:12–14 NIV

In 1 Samuel we discover the story of Hannah, who struggled with infertility. She waited years to conceive a child. Today's scripture shows her at the temple, pouring her heart out to God, begging Him to fulfill her dream of a son. Her plea to the Lord was so passionate that Eli the priest actually thought she was drunk. Hannah respectfully corrected him, but she was weary with waiting, nearing the point of giving up.

Maybe you've been there. You've been waiting for a husband or a child or a raise or a healthy body. You're weary with begging for the same thing, day in and day out. Will God ever come through for you? Or should you just stop asking?

Don't stop asking! Even if your prayers sound like a drunk woman's, don't give up. Let your passion flow. Let your heart be heard. God wants you to keep trusting, keep believing, and keep standing strong, though you haven't yet seen the fulfillment of your dream.

What are you waiting on today? Don't give up.

I won't give up, Lord. If Hannah could hang in there, I can too. Give me courage to keep going. Amen.

God Always Comes Through

We remember before our God and Father your work produced by faith, your labor prompted by love, and your endurance inspired by hope in our Lord Jesus Christ.
1 THESSALONIANS 1:3 NIV

Sarah glanced down at her watch. The movie would start in two minutes. Where was her daughter?

Kelly often ran late, and this time was no different. Sarah waited a few more minutes, then finally went into the theater to check the crowd. It was going to be difficult to find two seats together. As the opening credits rolled, Sarah slipped into a seat right under the screen.

Twenty minutes later, Kelly texted her mom to say she was in the lobby. Sarah had to leave her seat, walk out with Kelly's ticket, and usher her daughter back inside, all while quietly explaining what she'd missed to that point.

People who hold things up can be annoying, can't they? And it's really a drag to cover for someone who's perpetually late.

Thankfully, God is never late. His timetable is perfect, whether or not we realize that in the moment. We never need to doubt that He'll come through for us. He always does. Yes, sometimes it's at the eleventh hour. But don't worry—the movie is just starting.

I'll wait on You, Lord, no matter how long.
Even in the eleventh hour, I'll keep holding on. Amen.

Waiting for the Harvest

"At harvest time he sent a servant to the tenants to collect from them some of the fruit of the vineyard."
MARK 12:2 NIV

Cora put several tomato plants into her little garden and waited for them to produce. For the longest time it seemed like they wouldn't. Finally, one day she discovered tiny buds. Those morphed into little green balls that eventually became full-grown tomatoes. They stayed green for a spell, and then. . .*bam!* Red, juicy tomatoes, ripe for the picking.

Think about Cora's tomato plants in light of your spiritual journey. What if she had plucked those tiny buds before they grew into tomatoes? Or if she'd snatched off the tomatoes before they were ripe? Would they have been of any value?

No doubt we've all been there a time or two. We get tired of waiting, so we're tempted to pluck fruit from the vine before its time. We know the outcome will be bitter, but we just can't wait any longer.

Wait longer anyway. Watch as God develops and transforms your situation, blossoming it into a thing of real beauty. A bitter piece of fruit is just bitter. Wait until it's ready. You'll enjoy it then and remember it forever.

The harvest is coming, Lord. I can feel it. I'll keep waiting. I can trust You in the in-between times. Amen.

His Yoke Is Easy

"Take my yoke upon you, and learn from me, for I am gentle and lowly in heart, and you will find rest for your souls."
MATTHEW 11:29 ESV

In Bible days, oxen were yoked together to work in a field. Working together, the animals were able to accomplish more. The yoke's weight was evenly distributed and divided the strain of the work. It protected both the oxen and the man leading them.

That's what God has in mind with His "yoke." His burden is lighter than anything the world will throw on you. We've all tried to do things our own way, but (no surprise here) He has the better way.

Sure, it might seem cumbersome to be yoked to God. But we've seen how far we get when we try to plow ahead alone. Accept Jesus' yoke and watch as He carries the load. You can pass your burdens off to Him today. Simply say, "Jesus, I'm tired. I'm weary with carrying this load. I yoke myself to You and ask You to take my burden." Guess what? He will!

Lord, I'm exhausted with trying to do things on my own. I'm worn out, in fact. So, I'll yoke myself to You. You're the best burden bearer ever! Amen.

Listen, You Stubborn-Hearted!

"Listen to me, you stubborn-hearted,
you who are now far from my righteousness."
ISAIAH 46:12 NIV

"It's my way or the highway." Maybe you know someone who says that. Maybe you've said it a time or two yourself! It's hard to be around people who demand you do everything their way. They get worked up into a lather if you don't immediately follow their lead. Demanding people have a way of wrecking our rest.

Let's face it—even though your boss has a right to tell you how to do something, it's better if she does so kindly. But this is a two-way street, friend. Take care never to be the person who demands that other people jump—and gets irritated when they don't immediately ask, "How high?" You don't want to be responsible for ruining someone else's rest.

Even if you think you're right, don't be harsh with your demands. Never allow your own pride to keep you from being teachable. "Stubborn-hearted" isn't an attractive trait for anyone—especially one of God's daughters.

I'm sorry for the times I've been stubborn and prideful, Lord. I've lost sleep over my own bad attitude. Temper me, I pray, and make me more like You. Amen.

Do It God's Way

So on the second day they marched around the city once and returned to the camp. They did this for six days.
JOSHUA 6:14 NIV

Many of us have our set ways of approaching trouble. When we run into a tricky situation, we already have a default reaction, a pre-planned approach for dealing with it. Problem is, our way doesn't always work, does it?

God's ways are—shall we say—*different*. Jesus rubbed mud on a blind man's eyes, remember? And in today's scripture, God told Joshua to march around enemy Jericho for seven days straight and then blow trumpets.

Seven days? What if you're on a tight schedule? No doubt many of us would say, "Lord, could we go to plan B?"

But His plan A is always the best. The blind man regained his sight. The city of Jericho fell. The best possible outcomes arise when we walk in step with God.

What strange thing is He asking you to do today? What are you arguing over? *Lord, I've got ten other ways to fix that problem! Do I have to do it Your way?*

Yes, you need to do it His way. When you finally submit to His will and ways, He'll lead you through to a lovely ending.

Okay, Lord. . .here we go! I'm doing it Your way, even if it means a little discomfort on my part. Help me, I pray. Amen.

Who Are You Trying to Please?

Am I now trying to win the approval of human beings, or of God? Or am I trying to please people? If I were still trying to please people, I would not be a servant of Christ.

GALATIANS 1:10 NIV

Let's face it—most of us are people pleasers. Oh, we say we're not. But when it comes right down to it, everyone wants to be loved, valued, and appreciated. No one wants to stick out like the proverbial sore thumb.

But here's a hard truth, one that might leave you scratching your head: Jesus *wants* you to stick out. He never meant for you to go along with the crowd.

Maybe you read that and say, "Ugh. I don't want that. It's so much easier to blend in." And you're right. It's easier, at least at first, to go along with the crowd rather than push back when the Spirit inside you is warning, "Don't do that!"

But when you follow people over God, you often wind up with your insides in a knot. You'll never find lasting peace because you can never please everyone all the time.

So seek to please God alone. It's His approval you need, and (don't miss this) *you already have it*. From the moment you accepted the sacrifice of His Son as a covering for your sins, you were spotless, perfect in the Father's sight.

Stop trying to satisfy people. You'll never succeed anyway. Follow hard after Jesus, and He'll give you a peace that passes all understanding.

I will seek to please You, Lord, not people. Help me, I pray. Amen.

A Strong Light

Your word is a lamp for my feet, a light on my path.
Psalm 119:105 NIV

Ever tried to walk across a room in the dark? You know how dangerous that can be. Accidents happen in the dark. Chaos takes place in the dark, whether physically or spiritually.

But God. . .

He's the one with the spotlight who can illuminate any dark path you're traveling. His Word is a lamp, or what we would think of today as a flashlight. In the dark, you take hesitant, tiny steps. . . but when you shine a strong light on the ground in front of you, you can clearly see what's coming. You can walk with confidence. This is why it's so important to stay in God's Word.

He has provided a light for your path. Though it's really *His* path. God has a way for you to walk in, one that may seem dark and scary at times but is totally within His knowledge and control. Settle that truth in your mind and you'll rest easier. You won't be as stressed out. Even when you hit bumps in the road, remember that God is still leading and guiding. He's never let you down before, and He never will.

Let God light your path! Go grab your Bible right now.

Thank You for the reminder that it's Your path, Jesus! Keep it well lit! Bring the Word to life in my heart, I pray! Amen.

What's Left Behind

"Peace I leave with you; my peace I give to you. Not as the world gives do I give to you. Let not your hearts be troubled, neither let them be afraid."

John 14:27 ESV

Sometimes, before leaving her young adult daughter's apartment, a mom will sneak a twenty-dollar bill into a spot that's not too obvious but also not hard to find. It's her way of wrapping up a visit with a final gift of love.

A few weeks after Jesus ascended to heaven, He sent His Holy Spirit back to earth. In essence, our Lord "left behind" a piece of Himself so His followers could have guidance, comfort, and peace. What a legacy!

Jesus gives. . .and gives. . .and gives some more. And He doesn't give the way the world does. When He shows His generosity, it's permanent. The peace He offers is no cheap counterfeit; it's the real deal. You know, from scripture and experience, that this is all true. You can rest easy in Him.

Lord, I'm so grateful You left behind Your Spirit. What a gift! I want to leave behind peace too. Help me be a legacy leaver, I pray. Amen.

It's Supernatural

"But you will receive power when the Holy Spirit has come upon you, and you will be my witnesses in Jerusalem and in all Judea and Samaria, and to the end of the earth."

ACTS 1:8 ESV

It's supernatural.

That word *supernatural* is intriguing, isn't it? When people use the term, they're saying, "It's above and beyond the realm of the natural." In other words, you couldn't have pulled it off yourself.

God's peace is supernatural. It's definitely above and beyond the realm of the natural. In fact, it's so far beyond you might wonder how it's possible at all. And yet, God sends His peace, right in the middle of the storms you're experiencing.

Think about the Holy Spirit. He's the embodiment of peace. When you're filled with the Spirit of God, you receive all the power you need to let go of the angst. To release the pain. To enjoy rest and comfort. The Spirit is called "the Comforter," after all.

The Spirit gives power—to be comforted. What an amazing revelation!

Thank You, Lord, for the gift of Your Spirit. I know where my power comes from. I can live above and beyond the realm of the natural, experiencing supernatural comfort and peace in You. How grateful I am. Amen.

Jesus Has Already Done It

Jesus answered them, "Do you finally believe? In fact, you're about to make a run for it—saving your own skins and abandoning me. But I'm not abandoned. The Father is with me. I've told you all this so that trusting me, you will be unshakable and assured, deeply at peace. In this godless world you will continue to experience difficulties. But take heart! I've conquered the world."

JOHN 16:31–33 MSG

It seems like an elusive dream. Peace "feels" impossible, in light of what you're going through. And yet, according to today's scripture, it's not at all impossible. In fact, it's a promise straight from the heart of your adoring heavenly Father. He wants you to know that even in the midst of your chaos, He can calm your thoughts. He can calm your heart. He can even temper your tongue. (Hallelujah!) God can saturate you with His Spirit in a way that restores order where there was chaos just moments before.

Sure, you'll have tough times. They're inevitable. But Jesus has conquered the world. Think about that: Whatever you're fretting over right now, in this very moment, is just a small part of the world that He has already overcome. He's not "going to" conquer the world. He already has—past tense.

You can rest easy in Him. There's no need to run. Trusting Jesus brings you through the chaos unshaken and assured, deeply at peace. Amen?

Okay, I see how this works now, Lord. You've already taken care of everything. I simply have to rest in You. Please help me to do that. Amen.

You Can't Escape!

Where can I go from your Spirit? Where can I flee from your presence? If I go up to the heavens, you are there; if I make my bed in the depths, you are there. If I rise on the wings of the dawn, if I settle on the far side of the sea, even there your hand will guide me, your right hand will hold me fast.

PSALM 139:7–10 NIV

You can't escape God. His Spirit is literally everywhere.

Madison wasn't sure she believed that. She'd gone through a horrible season in life and decided to hide away—from everyone and everything. Madison even tried to hide from God, hoping that some serious "me time" would solve her problems.

But you can't outrun God. His Spirit follows you, which is why the nineteenth-century English poet Francis Thompson called Him "the Hound of Heaven."

If you can't hide from the Lord, you really can't hide from His peace either. No matter what kind of path you walk, His peace is always within your reach. On the good days. On the bad days. At sunrise. At sunset. When you're surrounded on all sides by enemies. When you're lifting your hands in praise. No matter what or where, He's at your side, ready to pour out His peace.

You can't escape it, girl, so you might as well just let that peace saturate your heart, mind, and spirit!

I won't run! I won't hide! I'll draw close to You and accept that peace offering, Lord! Amen.

Stare It Down

You keep him in perfect peace whose mind is stayed on you, because he trusts in you.
ISAIAH 26:3 ESV

Perfect peace. Ever wonder what that would feel like? There are few (if any) perfect things in this world, so that's a big claim. But then again, God is a pretty big God! If anyone has a right to claim something is perfect, He does.

He wants to give you perfect peace. It's yours for the taking. But, as with any gift, it has to be accepted. And there is a certain condition to this gift: You need to keep your mind "stayed" on God. (Remember how you used to play that staring game with your friends, where you locked your eyes on each other until someone finally looked away? It's kind of like that.)

You can't hyper-focus on your problems and expect that gift-wrapped package of peace to open on its own. You have to look away from the chaos and fear and turn your gaze toward God and peace. Go ahead and stare at Him. He's saying, "Hey, there's a better way!"

Peace is the better way. It's the only way to finally find rest.

I'll keep my eyes on Your version of peace, Lord. I won't be distracted by the chaos of life. Amen.

Wings like a Dove

And I say, "Oh, that I had wings like a dove!
I would fly away and be at rest."
PSALM 55:6 ESV

Have you ever wondered what it would be like to be a bird, flying free up in the sky? How marvelous to soar with wings like an eagle. How delightful to rise into the air like a dove, to fly over your circumstances, and to land in a place far away from the chaos.

The writer of this psalm must have been pretty stressed out. And yet, in the stress, he penned a lovely thought: "Oh, that I had wings like a dove! I would fly away and be at rest."

No doubt you've felt like that. But we don't have wings. Instead, we crawl back into bed and pull the covers over our heads. Or slide into a hot bubble bath. Or fire up the car for a long drive, away from the kids, the boss, the headaches.

Stepping away from time to time is a healthy thing. You can't always get away, but a little escape—to the coffee shop, to your favorite store, to a nature trail—is a good way to forget your troubles for a bit.

Just remember that it's not enough to simply be alone. You have to get alone *with God*. Include Him in your solitude and seek His perspective on what you're going through. Then you can truly fly away and be at rest.

Oh, sometimes I wish I could fly away, Lord! Thank You for the reminder that I can. I can fly straight into Your arms for seasons of rest and refreshment. Amen.

Sheltered with His Wings

He will cover you with his feathers, and under his wings you will find refuge; his faithfulness will be your shield and rampart.
Psalm 91:4 NIV

Ever felt like hiding out? Ever wish you could just escape for a while, getting so far away that people and circumstances couldn't find you?

God knew you would have days like that. Perhaps that's why today's scripture is included in His Word. There will be days when you need shelter, a hiding place. And this verse says you can find that shelter under God's wings. He will protect you like a mother hen guards her chicks. You're covered by His feathers.

It's an interesting picture. Feathers protect a bird while also providing beauty. Under those features, which are not heavy things, you're not burdened. You're simply safe.

God's got you. He knows the problems you're going through, the thoughts tumbling through your head, the ache in your heart. He knows your anger, your worry, your fear. And He's perfectly willing to hide you away until you get it figured out. . .with His help, of course!

I'll hide away with You, Jesus. I'm safe under Your wings. Amen.

He's Got You Covered

"Make the interior of the sacred Tent, the Tent of my presence, out of ten pieces of fine linen woven with blue, purple, and red wool. Embroider them with figures of winged creatures."
EXODUS 26:1 GNT

Maybe you're one of those people who doesn't spend a lot of time in the Old Testament. Sure, some of its stories are harder to read. Just imagine what it must have been like to live under the old covenant!

But the Old Testament contains many glimpses of grace, things that point to the ultimate sacrifice for sin in Jesus Christ. When God commanded Moses to build the tabernacle, He gave very specific instructions about the "Holy of Holies," the particular part of the tabernacle that He planned to inhabit. When God inhabits a space, you know He cares deeply about it.

Well, guess what? Today He inhabits *you*! He lives inside every follower of Jesus.

Now reread today's scripture. Notice that God wanted figures of angels' wings sewn into the linen of the tabernacle. He wanted the people to remember that they were covered, shielded, protected.

And God is still covering us. Even now, you're safely guarded by heavenly beings. You're not only hidden under God's wings, you're surrounded by wings of angels!

What an amazing reminder, Lord! You've totally got me covered! I'm protected by You. Amen.

The Cleft of the Rock

"When my glory passes by, I will put you in a cleft in the rock and cover you with my hand until I have passed by."
EXODUS 33:22 NIV

Picture this: Moses is well into his adventure, leading the Hebrews to the Promised Land. God commends Moses, and in return the man asks to see the Lord's glory. Only one problem—scripture is clear that no one can look on the face of God and live. But Moses didn't seem to care about that part. He just wanted more of God.

So the Lord did something unique. He hid Moses in the cleft of a rock and then passed by, revealing only His back side. God knew that a human being could only take so much of His presence, His holiness, His perfection.

Maybe you're like Moses, in that you're ready for more. This would be a terrific day to hide yourself away in the "cleft of the rock"—that hidden space, away from the cares of life, where your viewpoint is limited. In that safe place, you're not skimming social media or paying bills. You have access to one thing—God Himself. When He shows up, watch out! His presence changes everything!

Lord, I'm ready. I want more of You. Like Moses, I choose to hide myself in the cleft of the rock, where I'm able to view Your glory! Come near me, I pray. Amen.

When You Want to Run

Where shall I go from your Spirit? Or where shall I flee from your presence? If I ascend to heaven, you are there! If I make my bed in Sheol, you are there! If I take the wings of the morning and dwell in the uttermost parts of the sea, even there your hand shall lead me, and your right hand shall hold me.

PSALM 139:7–10 ESV

As a kid, did you ever want to run away from home? Many kids do. Maybe they disagree with their parents' rules. Maybe Mom or Dad took a sibling's side in an argument. And the decision is made: "That's it! I'm done! I'm out of here." Some kids even pack a bag, but that's often where the big escape fizzles. Where to next? Would Grandmother take you in? Your best friend's mom, perhaps? Surely someone would understand.

Life gives us plenty of moments when we want to run. Whether it's a job or schooling or some relationship that is causing stress, the desire to abandon ship is the same. When you feel like running, go ahead—straight to the Lord. You can trust Him with whatever you're going through. He has the answers you need now as well as a plan to move you forward. You can't get away from His Spirit, and why would you want to? Run to God and hold that warm, protective, loving hand.

Instead of running away from You, I'll run toward You, Lord. When I'm afraid. When I'm feeling lost. When I'm confused. I'll run straight to Your arms for the answers only You can provide. Amen.

Our Bountiful Father

Return, O my soul, to your rest; for the LORD
has dealt bountifully with you.
PSALM 116:7 ESV

Sometimes we think of God as austere, like a harsh Father with a belt in His hand, ready to spank us for everything we've done wrong. But He's just the opposite. He's loving and gracious, a Father who—according to today's scripture—deals bountifully with us.

To understand this, let's consider the word *bountiful*. When a farmer has a bountiful crop, it's more than he expected. So our God is a "more than" kind of Father!

He's like a dad on Christmas morning, eager to lavish his kids with every good thing. Not just one or two gifts—no! He has a roomful of goodies. Why? Because he adores his children and can't wait to bless them.

That's how God feels about you, girl. He's a good, good Father who has dealt bountifully with you. And He longs for your soul to be at rest so that He can bless you even more.

Draw near to your Father today. Trust Him for His very best.

Lord, You've been so good to me. Forgive me for the times I've avoided You. I'll come running back today, Father, and I won't be afraid. Your bounty woos and wins me, every time. Amen.

Maker of All

There is for us only one God, the Father, who is the Creator of all things and for whom we live; and there is only one Lord, Jesus Christ, through whom all things were created and through whom we live.
1 CORINTHIANS 8:6 GNT

If you had to summarize today's scripture, you could simply say, "God is the Maker of all," the utterly unique, one-and-only Creator.

Unlike us, God is not tired or stressed by His duties. He was (and is) capable of doing all things. He made everything you see, including yourself. And He's the one working full-time to keep you alive. . .especially on the road, where all those crazy people are texting and driving.

God made all things, and it didn't weary Him a bit. We do what we do, and we're exhausted. That's okay—we're human. But aren't you glad you know and serve the almighty, all-knowing, all-loving Maker of the entire universe? Whatever troubles you is no match for Him. So give your stresses to God, because He can handle them. Then rest well tonight.

Lord, it's amazing to me that You made everything, see everything, and manage everything. What a magnificent God You are! I'm in awe of You! Amen.

Above and Beyond

Now to him who is able to do immeasurably more than all we ask or imagine, according to his power that is at work within us, to him be glory in the church and in Christ Jesus throughout all generations, for ever and ever! Amen.
EPHESIANS 3:20–21 NIV

God always goes above and beyond what we could ask or think. Don't believe it? Ask Annie. She was struggling with a computer issue. Her laptop needed to be replaced. She had no choice but to spend money on a new one.

Imagine her surprise a few days later when an unexpected check arrived in the mail—for exactly the amount of money she'd spent on the laptop. That couldn't be a coincidence. It had to be a God-incidence!

Some call such situations "God-winks." Hasn't He winked at you a time or two, going above and beyond what you would ever have guessed? Remember how excited you were in the moment? Don't let that excitement fade. He's going to do it again. . .and again. . . and again.

You can truly rest your soul in God, knowing that He stands ready to delight and amaze you in response to your trust.

I'll do it, Lord! I'll rest in You. You've got me covered. I can't wait to see what You have up Your sleeve, in fact! Amen.

Thanksgiving

Let us come before him with thanksgiving
and sing joyful songs of praise.
PSALM 95:2 GNT

What's your favorite Thanksgiving memory? Maybe it goes back to your childhood, around the table with grandparents, aunts, uncles, and cousins. Or maybe it was much more recent, a beautiful dinner with your own kids or your fiancé or some dear friends.

You know that it doesn't really matter *what* you're eating as long as you've gathered with friends and family. Part of the proverbial "bounty" of Thanksgiving is the fact that you're sharing a meal with people you love.

That's how it is in our relationship with God too. He satisfies our souls in much the same way turkey and dressing (or ham and potatoes or tacos and chips) fill us up at Thanksgiving. God gives you that more-than-enough feeling when you simply devote time to Him. He's so happy just to be with you.

If that doesn't lead to a restful spirit, what will? Come to the Lord with thanksgiving and joyful songs of praise!

Today I'm pausing to give thanks for Your bounty, Lord! You've surrounded me with Your presence and with others who love You too. How I praise and thank You! Amen.

Harvesttime

"Let both grow together until the harvest. At that time I will tell the harvesters: First collect the weeds and tie them in bundles to be burned; then gather the wheat and bring it into my barn."
MATTHEW 13:30 NIV

Think of a farmer bringing in the harvest. He's waited and waited and waited some more, until just the right moment when the crop is ready. He's been incredibly patient.

Finally, the day arrives. It's not going to be easy, but he's going to get that crop in, no matter what. The excitement of what he's worked for makes this final effort worthwhile. That, and he realizes how many lives he's going to impact as other people eat the food he's produced.

God has a bountiful harvest for us too. Like that farmer, we have to be patient until the right moment. Sometimes we wait for years. But God's timing is perfect and His results superb. Miracles are unfolding like the incredible process of seeds becoming plants and producing a crop.

Be patient. God has a harvest for you. Until then, rest easy. The farmer's not staying awake at night trying to will his crop into being. Neither should you.

Harvest is coming, Lord! You've planted seeds in my heart, and they've taken root. Now I get to watch them grow and develop into everything they were meant to be. I can't wait to see what You have in store for me. Amen.

Toss It His Way

Casting all your anxieties on him, because he cares for you.
1 PETER 5:7 ESV

Whether you ever played softball or not, the game offers a visual example for our Christian lives. Imagine being the pitcher, lobbing (or perhaps firing) the ball toward home plate. Now imagine the ball is your anxiety. You can toss your stresses all the way home! Jesus is happy to catch them and deal with them. He's the only one who really can, you know.

Here's the problem, though. Many of us *don't* cast our cares on Him. We drag them around with us, like weights we were meant to carry. But we never were called to slog through life that way. Jesus always intended for us to let them go, to pitch them straight into His hands.

What anxieties are weighing you down? Maybe it's time to warm up that pitching arm. Square up, look toward home, and cast all your anxieties on Him. Once you do? The sky's the limit!

I'll do it, Jesus! I'll cast my cares on You. It hardly seems fair to You to carry my struggles, but I know You're ready, willing, and able. Here they come! Amen.

Be Content

So be content with who you are, and don't put on airs. God's strong hand is on you; he'll promote you at the right time. Live carefree before God; he is most careful with you.
1 PETER 5:6–7 MSG

Have you ever considered the possibility that some of your unrest might grow out of discontentment? When you crave what other people have—whether homes or jobs or relationships or status—you're coveting. Sorry to put things so bluntly, but it's true!

Today, toss that discontentment to the curb. Get rid of it. Stop comparing yourself to others. Only then will you be free to understand what the word *contentment* really means.

Take another look at today's scripture. To be content means that you're genuinely okay with what you have. You're not putting on airs, trying to show off. Why should you? You're a child of the most high King! You're a princess! God has given you access to the keys to the kingdom. In other words, you already have everything you could possibly need.

You also have the promise that He'll take care of you. So when you find yourself feeling envious, stop and consciously tell yourself, "I have Jesus, and that's everything." You'll save yourself a lot of anxiety if you'll just place your trust in Him.

I'm learning to be content, Jesus. It's not always easy, especially when I see what others have. But I long to be fully content in You. Amen.

Soaring Above It

No temptation has overtaken you except what is common to mankind. And God is faithful; he will not let you be tempted beyond what you can bear. But when you are tempted, he will also provide a way out so that you can endure it.

1 CORINTHIANS 10:13 NIV

When you fly in an airplane, there's a fascinating moment shortly after takeoff when you pass through the clouds. From that point forward, you're looking down on the very things you used to stare up at!

Now picture that experience in light of the troubles that cloud your vision. They seem to loom large overhead, casting eerie shadows. But God wants to change your perspective. When you soar above your circumstances, you begin to see those problems for what they really are. They're nothing but wispy clouds floating on the wind.

How do you rise above your circumstances? By giving them to Jesus. He's ready and willing—eager, in fact—to handle everything for you. He'll free you up to soar higher and go farther!

You always provide a way out, Lord! I love that about You. When I'm facing gloomy circumstances, You give me wings to soar above them. I refuse to be bogged down in fear. I'll find rest for my soul by placing the situation in Your hands. Amen.

Letting Go

"Remember not the former things, nor consider the things of old. Behold, I am doing a new thing; now it springs forth, do you not perceive it? I will make a way in the wilderness and rivers in the desert."

ISAIAH 43:18–19 ESV

Imagine you're grabbing a casserole dish from the oven, but you forgot to don an oven mitt first. You touch the hot pan and instantly. . .what? Let go, of course! Your first instinct is to release your hand from the thing that causes pain.

When you go through tough seasons of life, remember that letting go is also for the best. But sometimes we hang on for dear life, nursing our problem like a favorite child.

God says, "Let it go." Drop it. Don't touch it again.

The only way to do that is to give the issue to Him. Let Him know, once and for all, that it's His. . .and His alone. You've tried to fix it. You've tried to tame it. You've tried to pretend it's not as big as it really is. But nothing is working. God will. He's big enough. He's strong enough. He's patient and loving and powerful enough.

So let it go. Once you do, you'll find the rest for your soul that has so far escaped you.

Okay, Lord. . .I'm letting go, once and for all. I'm sorry I've held things in such a tight grip till now. Show me how to release my pains, problems, and emotions into Your control. Amen.

Oversharing?

Whoever guards his mouth preserves his life;
he who opens wide his lips comes to ruin.
PROVERBS 13:3 ESV

Geena was good at getting rid of her problems. She shared them with her friends, dumping every detail on them. She spilled them on her husband, covering him with every juicy nugget. She called her mom with regular reports, not missing one tiny part of the story. Over and over it would go with each person Geena knew.

There was only one problem: She wasn't really "getting rid of" her problems. That's a completely different thing than spreading them around.

Maybe you know what that's like. You're having a hard time getting over some issue, but you can't figure out why. You've shared it with a trusted friend. You've asked your husband for his opinion. You've opened up to a coworker. But the problem just isn't going away.

Maybe it's time to stop tossing it to people and start tossing it to God. Oversharing is never a problem for Him. In fact, the more you tell God, the better. He loves it when you open up. (Just be sure to listen for His still, small response.)

Here I am, Lord, ready to share my heart with You.
I've already dumped it on everyone else.
Sorry I waited so long to come to You. Amen.

Power to the Weary

He gives power to the faint, and to him who has no might he increases strength.
Isaiah 40:29 ESV

Aren't you glad for this biblical promise? God gives power to the faint. He searches for the child who has no strength and provides a boost. It's spiritual yeast to our otherwise flat bread. All the energy, all the power, comes from Him.

Picture yourself at the gym. Your trainer is standing by. You want to please him, but you're not feeling it today. You drag yourself from one piece of equipment to the next, but every step is a chore. Then he says something so kind and complimentary that you're infused with a new energy. You're like a new person, in fact. Now you bound from workout to workout, ready to prove you've got the goods.

Where did that energy come from? A minute earlier you were wiped out. The wherewithal to begin again came from a word of encouragement.

God uses all sorts of people and experiences to supernaturally invigorate us with His power. Who or what has He used in your life? Think you could pass that along to someone else?

Thank You for giving power to the faint, Lord! You've used so many people and experiences to give me the strength I need! How grateful I am. Amen.

Plug In!

"But you will receive power when the Holy Spirit has come upon you, and you will be my witnesses in Jerusalem and in all Judea and Samaria, and to the end of the earth."
ACTS 1:8 ESV

Sally fussed and fumed as she tried to get her blow-dryer to work. She pushed every button. Then she thought to make sure it was plugged in. (It was.) This thing was only six months old. The thought of buying a new one was irritating. But what could she do?

Oh. . .she could push that little red RESET button on the wall outlet.

Voilà! Power! At last!

Maybe that's happened to you. You thought a computer, a phone, a curling iron had died, only to discover that the source of power was interrupted.

That's how it is when we stop spending time with God. The usual flow seems to dry up. We don't have the energy to do what we once did. Then we realize we've disconnected from our source. No wonder we're drained! No wonder we can't summon the wherewithal to get things done.

Plug back in. Hit the RESET button. Without an uninterrupted line to heaven, you'll be sapped in a hurry!

I offer myself to You again today, Lord! Give me the power I need to get things done. I'll rest easy, knowing You are my source. Amen.

Pace Yourself

So let's not allow ourselves to get fatigued doing good. At the right time we will harvest a good crop if we don't give up, or quit. Right now, therefore, every time we get the chance, let us work for the benefit of all, starting with the people closest to us in the community of faith.

GALATIANS 6:9–10 MSG

Have you ever gotten fatigued doing good? Maybe you lead a women's Bible study group, teach a Sunday school class, or serve as a stay-at-home mom completely devoted to your kids, husband, and house. It's possible to be exhausted doing all sorts of great deeds.

God wants you to be a good-deed doer. But remember, with Him you don't have to prove anything. You don't have to work around the clock to show Him you've got what it takes.

Of course, that's the way the world does it. And that's the attitude that results in fatigue. But God has a better way. He wants you to do the right thing but also to pace yourself as you move steadily forward. That way you won't be tempted to give up due to exhaustion.

One step at a time. One day at a time. Just keep on keeping on.

I get it, Jesus. I wear myself out when I go too hard and fast. Help me pace myself, I pray. Amen.

Soul Provider

"You shall love the LORD your God with all your heart and with all your soul and with all your might."
DEUTERONOMY 6:5 ESV

Love the Lord your God with all your *soul*. What is your soul, anyway?

Most would say that your "soulish" areas are your heart, mind, and emotions. They're certainly interconnected. Your heart often controls your thoughts. What you feel often drives your thinking. So if these things are out of alignment, or if you're too exhausted to "feel" or "think" properly, nothing seems to work right. If your emotions are out of whack, everything is affected. Troubles seem greatly exaggerated. Worries increase. Poor decisions are made.

Now you see why it's so critical to rest your soul in God. Those emotions? They can be at rest. That aching heart? It can rest too. And those thoughts that swirl through your brain? They can be calmed and controlled when you know God is in charge.

Today, consciously and intentionally give your soul to Jesus. Commit to Him with all that you feel—or don't feel. With all that you think—or don't think. He created you and knows every part of you. . .mind, heart, and emotions.

Thank You for the reminder that my soul can be at rest, Lord! I'm grateful for the peace and comfort that only You can bring. Amen.

Don't Be Half-Hearted

"I know your deeds, that you are neither cold nor hot. I wish you were either one or the other! So, because you are lukewarm—neither hot nor cold—I am about to spit you out of my mouth."
REVELATION 3:15–16 NIV

Maybe today's verses don't seem to fit in a book called *Devotions to Quiet Your Soul.* The scripture is about work. And it describes Jesus criticizing and even threatening His followers!

But think of it this way: When do you sleep the best? Isn't it after you've really worked hard? That's probably why Solomon wrote, "The sleep of a laborer is sweet" (Ecclesiastes 5:12 NIV).

So if you're working hard for Jesus—not half-hearted, but hot for His glory—a rest will follow. Check out Hebrews 4 for that promise.

Then what about Jesus' harsh words in Revelation 3? Well, He is the Lord of the universe. He *deserves* our utmost effort. And after we've expended our best energies for Him, we'll be able to rest knowing that we've honored Him—not to be saved, but simply to show our love and appreciation for all He's done for us.

I'm sorry for my lukewarm state, Jesus. Stir me to action, I pray. Amen.

God's Not Worried

And behold, there arose a great storm on the sea, so that the boat was being swamped by the waves; but he was asleep.
MATTHEW 8:24 ESV

Do you enjoy thunderstorms? How about thunderstorms when you're trying to sleep?

One time Jesus and His disciples were on a boat on the Sea of Galilee. Taking advantage of a quiet moment, the Lord decided to sneak in a siesta. While He was snoozing, a wild storm blew in.

Jesus slept great. The disciples were in a panic. So they chose to wake their leader, to make sure He knew what was happening. As if the Creator of the universe would be unaware. . .

Here's an important truth: When you're going through storms, God is at peace. When you're in a tizzy, He's not rushing around trying to decide what to do. He's not worked up at all. Think about it—God has seen far worse situations than anything we experience.

He's not worried. Nor should you be. He's not panicking, so follow His lead. Just place your storm in His very capable hands. As the old song goes, He's got the whole world there.

I trust You, Lord. You've got this. I can rest easy, knowing You're not panicked. Amen.

His Wraparound Presence

Truly he is my rock and my salvation;
he is my fortress, I will never be shaken.
Psalm 62:2 niv

Fortress, castle, stronghold, defense—different translations use different words to describe God in today's scripture. Or, as one modern Bible version (tpt) puts it, God's "wraparound presence" always protects us. What an image!

Picture yourself on an ice-cold day. Though you'd rather be sitting in front of a fireplace, you have to be outside in the weather. Unfortunately, your coat's a little too small—maybe it goes back to your youth, or maybe you've gained a few pounds. . .and you simply can't get the thing buttoned! Now, because there's an exposed area, you're freezing. Though most of your body is covered, that one exposed area makes you vulnerable.

You never have to worry about that in the spiritual realm. God's got you wrapped up securely. He's always ready to cover you, to defend you, to be your champion.

Worry need never paralyze you. When God's presence surrounds you like a tailored coat, there's no room inside for anxiety. No matter how the cold winds blow, He's got you covered—in every sense of the word!

I'm so grateful You've got me surrounded, Lord! You're my safe place, my shelter from the storm. I can rest easy, knowing my champion defender is on the job! Amen.

No Fear in the Night

You will never worry about an attack of demonic forces at night nor have to fear a spirit of darkness coming against you.
PSALM 91:5 TPT

What a fascinating scripture! "You will never worry about an attack of demonic forces at night."

How many times have you tossed and turned at night, feeling like you're being attacked? And yet, as a blood-bought child of the King, you don't need to fret. When you rest your soul in Jesus, when you give yourself completely to His care, He steps in and takes over. Nothing can harm you with that kind of bodyguard.

Nor do you need to "fear a spirit of darkness coming against you." We all know that feeling of impending doom. But when anxiety threatens to wrap you in its fearsome tentacles, you can look it squarely in the eye and say, "Nope—you have no authority here! I'm a child of the King!"

There are privileges to being part of the royal family. A princess doesn't have to lie awake at night fretting over battles outside the castle. She's at peace, knowing the King is on the throne and His armies on guard. You never need to worry.

I trust You, Jesus! I can rest easy in You, letting go of the fear of night. I'm privileged to be Your child and so grateful for this special relationship we share. Amen.

When the Wicked Seem to Prosper

Don't envy evil people, and don't be jealous of the wicked.
PROVERBS 24:19 NCV

Lori's best friend was going through a horrible divorce. Her husband was abusive, especially after drinking too much. He just couldn't be trusted. But when the court date arrived, he showed up in his nicest suit, exuding good manners. Lori was disgusted to see him bluff the judge, who passed down a bad ruling.

Maybe you've walked through a situation like that. When injustices come—and they do from time to time—there's really only one thing you can do: give the whole frustrating mess to God. Those issues that aren't revealed in a courtroom or at the office or in your kid's school will come out eventually, in God's own time and ways.

Never assume the story is over. Never think that God is unaware. He has plot twists you can't even imagine. So hang on. . .don't worry. . .trust Him. He will ultimately make everything right.

I'm doing my best to be patient, Lord! I get so worked up when I see injustices. Help me to trust You— Your will, Your way, and Your timing. Amen.

It's All His

"Yours, O Lord, is the greatness and the power and the glory and the victory and the majesty, for all that is in the heavens and in the earth is yours. Yours is the kingdom, O Lord, and you are exalted as head above all."

1 Chronicles 29:11 ESV

What do you suppose God is doing right now, in the very midst of your worry-fest? Is He pacing heaven, trying to figure out what to do? Is He concerned about your adversaries? Or is He, as today's scripture indicates, in complete control?

If it's true that the Creator of heaven and earth holds all power and glory and victory, why should we fret? If it's really His kingdom and if He's really exalted as head above all, why do we toss and turn at night, trying to figure out what to do?

Here's a simple but profound truth you've already seen throughout this book: God's got this. All of heaven and earth is His. That means *you* are His. It means your problems are His. It means your adversaries are His.

It's all God's. And you can rest easy, knowing that the one who created and owns everything sees your situation. He cares deeply about you. Today, put your trust in the only one with the power to fix what you're going through.

It's all Yours, Lord! Why should I worry? Today I choose to trust in the one who owns it all. You're bigger than my problem, God! I'll rest in that truth. Amen.

I Won't Be Shaken

For God alone my soul waits in silence; from him comes my salvation. He alone is my rock and my salvation, my fortress; I shall not be greatly shaken.
Psalm 62:1–2 ESV

Have you ever literally felt your knees shake? Janie knew that feeling well. As a ten-year-old, she took part in her first piano recital. Janie was so nervous that when she reached for the pedal of the grand piano, her foot started bobbing up and down. The clacking noise that resulted only added to her nerves! Somehow, Janie made it through her piece, but then she ran from the stage, determined never to go through that trauma again.

Eventually Janie faced her fears and went on to play in many public events. She didn't allow her discomfort to permanently affect her. . .and, as Christians, neither should we.

No matter how unraveled we feel, God is never shaken. So He tells us to wait in silence on Him. He's our rock—steady, strong, and firm. He's our fortress, our strong tower, our defense. He's not shaking! And in His presence, our shaking diminishes.

Lord, I'm trusting the one who's never shaken! Thank You, my rock. Amen.

A Changing Message

When I felt secure, I said, "I will never be shaken."
PSALM 30:6 NIV

Today's verse is intriguing. The psalmist writes that when he felt secure, he said, "I will never be shaken." This begs the question: What did he say when he *didn't* feel secure?

It's so easy to say, "Wow, I'm blessed and highly favored!" when everything is going right. But the minute things begin to crumble, we change our message. We grumble and complain. We question God. We forget what He's already done for us. It's as if we lose our ability to remember good things from the past and can only summon up fear and anxiety. We get shaken.

Let's be consistent in our message, even during troubling times. We are always secure in God, no matter what we're walking through. We don't have to give way to fear.

Look at today's scripture one more time. There's a very telling word buried in there, one that's easy to overlook: *felt*.

We can't run on feelings. They'll get us into trouble every time. That's why it's critical to consciously place our trust in God. Why not take a moment to do that right now?

I won't trust my feelings, Lord. They've failed me before.
May I be consistent in my message of faith and hope,
even when chaos is swirling and troubles abound. Amen.

Shaken. . .*But!*

We are hard pressed on every side, but not crushed; perplexed, but not in despair; persecuted, but not abandoned; struck down, but not destroyed.
2 Corinthians 4:8–9 niv

Snow globes are so fun to shake, shake, shake. Don't you just love watching the flakes of fake snow swirling around inside? And how fascinating to note that the scene at the bottom—whatever it might be—remains steady and still. The shaking doesn't affect the little people or buildings because they're securely attached to the base.

Life can be like that snow globe. An unexpected tragedy shakes, shakes, shakes you to your core. How well you handle it depends on how deeply rooted you are. Just like characters or structures in the snow globe, you can come through this unscathed. Sure, you'll feel the swirling around you, but you won't be destroyed.

Look again at today's scripture: You are pressed down by troubles, *but*. You're not crushed.

You are perplexed, *but*. You're not abandoned.

You are struck down, *but*. You're not destroyed.

Woman of God, you will be shaken. But your heavenly Father will never let you fall.

Thank You, Lord, for the but! *I've been so badly shaken. I've been through so much. But I'm grateful for Your intervention. You hold me steady, Lord. Amen.*

Jesus Understands

We do not have a high priest who is unable to empathize with our weaknesses, but we have one who has been tempted in every way, just as we are—yet he did not sin.

Hebrews 4:15 NIV

Guilt is a thief. It steals our peace, our hope, and our rest. When we've done something wrong—or even just think we might have—guilt creeps through the shadows of our mind, snatching up our joy and leaving us feeling vulnerable. What can we do?

We look to Jesus. He understands. Not because He ever sinned, but because He was certainly tempted to. As the second member of the Trinity, Jesus never fell for Satan's traps the way we often do. But He understands the pressure, the weight, the burden of temptation, and He is ready and willing to help us through it. He's even happy to forgive us after we've failed.

If these truths don't ease our minds and allow us to rest easier, what will? Our Lord is able to empathize with everything that troubles us. And He's powerful enough to see us through. Whatever is stressing you now, girl, give it to Him. Jesus understands.

Lord, I'm so grateful for Your understanding, Your empathy, Your love. May I rest easy in You, my great high priest! Amen.

Stick with the Guide

I have set the LORD always before me;
because he is at my right hand, I shall not be shaken.
PSALM 16:8 ESV

So here's an admittedly extreme example: Picture yourself on a tour of the Amazon jungle, one of those excursions people pay big money for. Somehow, you've gotten separated from your guide. You're lost and all by yourself. . .well, separated from people, at least. The buzzing of insects and the cries of strange animals surround you. Your knees are knocking and your palms are sweating. You're afraid to call out for fear of attracting some unfriendly, very possibly hungry beast.

Life can be like that—a wild jungle full of frightening experiences, and all the worse when you're on your own. That's why we need to stick close to our guide, our strong and loving Lord. Without Him, there's no rest in your soul. Instead, you are filled with fear and turmoil.

Your guide knows the way. He knows how to deal with whatever dangers arise. And He cares deeply about what happens to you.

Stick with Him. Rest in Him.

You're the best guide ever, Jesus. I'm going to stick with You! Amen.

Satisfied

"I will satisfy the weary soul, and
every languishing soul I will replenish."
JEREMIAH 31:25 ESV

Miranda pushed her chair back from the table and stood. She reached for her empty plate that a half hour earlier was loaded with Thanksgiving favorites—turkey, dressing, mashed potatoes, green bean casserole, cranberry sauce. She'd eaten every bite and was full, but she hadn't overdone it. Carrying her plate to the sink, she thought, *That's the way a holiday meal should be. I am satisfied.*

As a well-prepared Thanksgiving meal satisfies our stomachs, so time with Jesus satisfies our souls. No matter how empty we've been, He fills the void. No matter how long our exhausting journey has been, He provides refreshment. Is your soul weary and languishing? Run to your Lord. He will satisfy you.

You fill me up, Lord! There's nothing else I need once I've spent time with You. You satisfy me in every possible way, and I'm grateful. Thank You, my all-sustaining God. Amen.

A Light to End the Night

Satisfy us in the morning with your steadfast love,
that we may rejoice and be glad all our days.
PSALM 90:14 ESV

One paraphrase of this verse begins, "Let the sunrise of your love end our dark night" (TPT). Isn't that what God does? His love truly is like the sunrise, breaking through the darkness we've faced.

Mari wasn't sure she would ever see sunlight again. A long battle with cancer had her feeling as if the darkness would swallow her whole. She dragged herself from appointment to appointment, from hospitalization to hospitalization. It felt overwhelming, but God was there. When she was finally declared cancer-free, it was truly like morning had come.

But maybe you never got the good report. Maybe your loved one didn't make it. Grief surrounds you like the shadows of night. Even then God can and will break through like the dawn. He can satisfy your heart and fill you with songs of joy, no matter how dark the night has been. There is always a dawn. . .and God will be there to satisfy your soul.

Jesus, please break through my clouded dawn!
Please show up soon to light the skies. Give me the
hope I need, and let me rest in You. Amen.

Pajama Days

And he said, "My presence will go with you, and I will give you rest."
EXODUS 33:14 ESV

Have you ever had a "pajama day" when you just never got out of your warmest, comfiest sleepwear? Those days are wonderful, aren't they? You're not focused on the outside world. You're taking the day off.

And you deserve it! You've worked hard. You've stayed the course in spite of the obstacles. And you're tired. In fact, you passed "wiped out" awhile back. You're "plumb tuckered out," as your grandma might have said.

So go ahead and kick your feet up. Take a bubble bath. Enjoy your alone time—with Jesus. Make sure He's part of your special day now so that tomorrow you'll have the wherewithal to face the next challenge. His presence gives you rest. He's knocking on your door right now—be sure you invite Him in.

I need a day to myself, Lord. . .a day with You.
Thank You for the rest I find in Your presence. Amen.

Contentment in Him

Not that I am speaking of being in need, for I have learned in whatever situation I am to be content. I know how to be brought low, and I know how to abound. In any and every circumstance, I have learned the secret of facing plenty and hunger, abundance and need. I can do all things through him who strengthens me.

PHILIPPIANS 4:11–13 ESV

Kennedi had a vague sense of dissatisfaction. She couldn't put her finger on it, but she was discontented most of the time. On the job. In her friendships. With her home. Even in her marriage.

She felt this keenly at church, where she struggled to fit in. And she had always wrestled with her weight, her looks, her ever-changing figure. She hated the nagging sensation that nothing was ever good enough.

Maybe you can relate. You're struggling with dissatisfaction too. It's clouding your thoughts and emotions.

God reminds you today that you can be fully satisfied in *Him*. When you look to other things—including people—to find satisfaction, you'll come up empty every time. But when you see the Lord as your only source, a supernatural satisfaction will follow.

A dissatisfied person will never truly be at rest. When you're content in God, though? You'll find peace and rest as never before.

I choose to be satisfied in You, Jesus. I won't seek satisfaction from people or things. I'll stick with You, Lord, and find rest. Amen.

Even There

"And the LORD *will guide you continually and satisfy your desire in scorched places and make your bones strong; and you shall be like a watered garden, like a spring of water whose waters do not fail."*
ISAIAH 58:11 ESV

Here we have a biblical promise that God won't just satisfy us on the good days. He will fill our hearts even when we're in the "scorched places." Even there, He'll make our bones strong.

Are you in a scorched place right now? Maybe you've been abandoned or hurt by someone you trusted. Your heart is twisted up and you're feeling hopeless.

Even there, dear woman.

Even there, God will satisfy your desire and make you strong. Even there you will be like a watered garden, like an unfailing spring. What a promise!

Even there, in the darkness. Even there, in the battle. Even there, in the depths of despair. Even when you're absolutely sure you can't take one step forward, you will. You'll take two. Or three. Or a thousand.

God will meet you there. And when He does, He will not only satisfy your soul, He will give you the energy and joy you need to see this thing through to the end. That's how much He loves you.

Thank You, Jesus! I'll meet You there, in the middle of my distress and pain. Amen.

Overcomer

"I have said these things to you, that in me you may have peace. In the world you will have tribulation. But take heart; I have overcome the world."
John 16:33 ESV

Have you ever climbed a big hill? You finally reach the top, then come back down the other side where you breathe a sigh of relief. *Whew!* To come over an obstacle like that is a challenge.

God wants you to "come over" (or *overcome*) all the obstacles life throws your way. Yes, the climb will be a challenge. But once you've made it to the other side of the financial crisis. . .or illness. . .or relationship challenge. . .you'll be so happy you persevered. Of course, you're only guaranteed victory in Jesus' strength.

He has overcome the world. He's already climbed that mountain. He's been to the top and come down the other side, all with you in mind. He's seen everything, and He knows the truth: There will be tribulation in your life. He faced it too. But He overcame it all and will help you do the same.

Just give your troubles to Him. He'll help you up and over the mountain—even if He needs to carry you on His shoulders.

I'll give my trials to You, Jesus. They're too big for me to handle. May I never forget that I'll be victorious only because You have already overcome the world. Amen.

How to Conquer

Every God-born person conquers the world's ways.
The conquering power that brings the world to its knees is our faith. The person who wins out over the world's ways is simply the one who believes Jesus is the Son of God.

1 JOHN 5:4–5 MSG

If, going into an athletic competition, you knew that you could come out a winner by simply following a well-documented plan, would you? Of course you would.

God's Word offers you such a plan. It starts with bowing your knee to the Creator of all things and listening for His still, small voice. As you do, His Spirit comes to reside inside you. And with that Spirit comes an amazing gift—power.

Maybe you've forgotten or never quite understood this reality. Maybe you're still trying to do things the world's way. But remember this: "The conquering power that brings the world to its knees" is your faith. Nothing more, nothing less.

To win in this life, just place your trust in God. Believe Jesus is the Son of God. Allow the Holy Spirit to fill, guide, and empower you.

Want to be a winner? Now you know the plan.

With You on my side, I am more than a conqueror, Jesus! I won't do things the world's way anymore. I'm following Your plan! Amen.

They Will Not Overcome You

"They will fight against you but will not overcome you, for I am with you and will rescue you," declares the Lord.

Jeremiah 1:19 NIV

Here's a verse with four—count 'em, *four*—promises in its twenty-two words. The promises are specific to Jeremiah, the young man God tapped to be His prophet to the rebellious people of Judah. But these truths are also found in other parts of scripture and can apply to us today too.

Promise #1: You will face opposition. That's the bad news. People will fight against us for any number of reasons. But Promise #2 is that they won't overcome us. Yes, our enemies can hurt us. They might even kill our bodies. But once you're in God's hands, you are safe for eternity.

Promise #3 is a preview of what Jesus Himself said just before He ascended back to heaven: "I am with you always, to the very end of the age" (Matthew 28:20 NIV). And Promise #4 may very well happen in this life. But if not, rescue will absolutely take place when God calls you home to heaven.

One promise of opposition and three of the victory God offers. That's a pretty good ratio!

Thank You for the promise that I won't be overtaken by the evil ones, Lord! I'm so grateful for the promise of Your presence and help. Amen.

A Wall of Bronze

"I will make you a wall to this people, a fortified wall of bronze; they will fight against you but will not overcome you, for I am with you to rescue and save you," declares the Lord.

Jeremiah 15:20 NIV

We lose a lot of sleep over the fear of what could happen. Because we don't have the ability to see the future, we often expect the worst. We picture bad things ahead.

But look at today's scripture. The Lord told His prophet Jeremiah that he would be "a wall" to the people—a fortified wall of bronze. They could come against Jeremiah all day long, but they wouldn't defeat him. The bronze wall would prevail every time.

As a child of God, you're a bronze wall too. The enemy can fire his arrows at you, but they'll just bounce off. Nothing can crush you, nothing can topple you, nothing can pry you away from your heavenly Father's loving care.

So stop fretting over what might appear around the bend. God is already there, ready to rescue and save. In the meantime, He's building you into a woman of great strength.

I'm a bronze wall, Lord! In You I am impenetrable! Thank You for that lovely image! Amen.

Upon This Rock

"I tell you that you are Peter, and on this rock I will build my church, and the gates of Hades will not overcome it."
MATTHEW 16:18 NIV

Picture Jesus (the Rock) saying to Peter (let's call him "Little Rock") that he's going to play a huge role in the building of the church. You could say that Peter was a chip off the old block.

What about you? Are you a chip off the old block? Are you part of the foundation of what God is doing on earth today? Are you making a difference, just as Jesus did? Or are you content to be just a pebble on the side of the road, unnoticed and uninvolved?

Be a Little Rock yourself. When all of Jesus' Little Rocks work together, they'll be like a massive boulder. Remember, Jesus once said that His followers would do even greater works than He did (John 14:12).

You are a rock! Even if you feel like a wet noodle, you're a rock. Nothing can stand against you as long as you stand firm in Jesus.

Thank You, my Rock, for making me an integral part of Your work. I want to make a difference in the world. Link me with other rocks, that together we might be a people of great strength! Amen.

Glass Half Full

He who dwells in the shelter of the Most High will abide in the shadow of the Almighty. I will say to the LORD, "My refuge and my fortress, my God, in whom I trust."
PSALM 91:1–2 ESV

Jenni had a hard time keeping things positive. She was sort of a naysayer, a glass-half-empty type of gal. Negativity ruled the day. Whether she was discussing the weather, her job, or her marriage, she always saw the worst. And, as a result, she usually ended up with it.

It's possible to talk yourself into a deep, dark place if you're not careful. Before you know it, those negative words become a self-fulfilling prophecy, one you never really wanted. And then your thoughts grow even darker because now the glass seems even emptier than before.

Words matter. When you pray to God, speak in faith, even if you have only a little. A mustard seed's worth is enough to quicken your heart and bring hope to a hopeless situation. Faith is a gift from God Himself, exercised by your will.

Speak in faith, girl.

I'll do my best to speak in faith, Lord. I want to be a glass-half-full kind of gal! Amen.

Mountain Mover

He replied, "Because you have so little faith. Truly I tell you, if you have faith as small as a mustard seed, you can say to this mountain, 'Move from here to there,' and it will move. Nothing will be impossible for you."
MATTHEW 17:20 NIV

"Why does it matter what I say?" you may ask. "So I grumble a little. I complain a little. I swear a little. I gossip a little. So what?"

Let's consider those questions in light of today's scripture.

Jesus told His followers that they could tell a mountain, "Move from here to there," and it would obey.

What if they looked at that mountain and said nothing? Then what? Or what if they looked at the mountain and said, "Ain't no way! I can't take that down!" What would happen?

What you say matters a lot. When you speak, you're reminding yourself (and all the powers of darkness) of what God is capable of doing. And He's capable of a lot! He's the great mountain mover, after all.

Watch your tongue. Use it for good. Go move some mountains!

I get it, Lord! I'll do my best to speak only faith-filled words that honor You. Help me, I pray. Amen.

Seasoned with Salt

Let your speech always be gracious, seasoned with salt,
so that you may know how you ought to answer each person.
COLOSSIANS 4:6 ESV

You didn't mean to snap at her. The words just slipped out. Now you regret them, and you're struggling to get past it. You're beating yourself up, in fact.

The Lord demands that we love others the way He loves us because He knows the ugly results of our failure. Unloved people struggle in so many ways. What a kinder world we'd enjoy if we simply adopted the "love as I love" motto of our Savior.

You'll rest easier—and so will your family and friends—if you season your words with salt. That is, *before you speak*, take a moment and think about what you want to say versus what you should say. Salt preserves and adds flavor. . .and so should your words.

If you commit to that pause, God will guard and guide your tongue. And the world will be an ever-so-slightly better place.

Guard my tongue, Jesus! Season my words with spiritual salt. I want to love people the way You've loved me. Show me how, I pray. Amen.

Health to the Body

Gracious words are like a honeycomb, sweetness to the soul and health to the body.
PROVERBS 16:24 ESV

Has anyone ever offered you a gracious word? Maybe you were battling low self-esteem when someone mentioned she loved your hair. Those little nuggets are pure gold, aren't they?

The Bible describes them as a honeycomb. They sweeten the soul—your heart, mind, emotions, and will—and bring health to your body.

Are you thinking, *Really? Words can affect my health?* It's true. What we hear affects our psychological state and our psychological state directly affects our health. Ask anyone with high blood pressure—arguments and angry words certainly aggravate that condition.

So speak gracious words over others. Offer compliments like the sweet gift they are. You'll bring rest and peace to many souls. . . including your own.

I'll watch what I say, Lord, and do my best to offer sweet words. May they be like honeycomb to the hearer! Amen.

Mouth and Heart

Let the words of my mouth and the meditation of my heart be acceptable in your sight, O Lord, my rock and my redeemer.

Psalm 19:14 ESV

You want to please your heavenly Father in everything. Sometimes, though, you worry that you're not. You make mistakes. You choose to sin. Sure, He loves you anyway. . .but you're still disappointed when you fail.

Everyone fails, so don't be too hard on yourself. But do pay attention.

Start by guarding your words. If you want to bring joy to your Father's heart (and peace to your own), temper your tongue. Let the words of your mouth and the meditation of your heart be acceptable to God.

Think about today's scripture: The words of your mouth and the meditation of your heart are two different things. People can hear your words, but they can't read your heart. Except that, "out of the abundance of the heart the mouth speaks" (Matthew 12:34 ESV). Now you see why it's so important to guard both.

I'll guard my heart and my mouth, Lord. May what comes out of both of them be acceptable in Your sight. Amen.

He Leads You

The LORD is my shepherd; I shall not want. He makes me lie down in green pastures. He leads me beside still waters.
PSALM 23:1–2 ESV

Maybe you've tried to take a pup on a walk with a leash. He has a mind of his own and doesn't want to follow your lead. He tries to chase every squirrel, car, or bicycle you pass. He barks at the trash truck and embarrasses you by yapping at the neighbor.

Dogs—and people—can be ornery, can't they? Something inside all of us balks at playing "following the leader." It just isn't much fun when you're the follower!

But following after Jesus. . .now that should be something else entirely. He will lead you with love and wisdom to a place of joy and peace. And all those times you pull at the proverbial leash, demanding your own way or yapping about every little thing, you're adding strain that was never meant to be.

Be an easy follower. Just stay close to Jesus and do what He says, and you'll have rest for your weary spirit. Don't take off on your own, convinced your plans are best. Truly commit to living your life *His* way. When you do, the results will be staggering. . .in a good way.

I trust You, Jesus. I want to follow closely and listen for Your instructions instead of forging a path on my own. Please help me! Amen.

Time in His Presence

It was in the year King Uzziah died that I saw the Lord. He was sitting on a lofty throne, and the train of his robe filled the Temple. Attending him were mighty seraphim, each having six wings. With two wings they covered their faces, with two they covered their feet, and with two they flew.

Isaiah 6:1–2 NLT

Sadie couldn't put her finger on why she felt restless—but she felt restless. Days were running together; they all felt the same. She didn't have the vigor for life that she'd had before. Things were just sort of. . .blah.

But when she went to a women's retreat, everything changed. The time in God's presence, surrounded by like-minded women, was just the ticket. There Sadie found spiritual rest. Her soul was reawakened. She began to dream again.

Something similar happened to Isaiah, an Old Testament prophet. He was in the temple when he saw the train of God's robe filling the room. His angels showed up in all their brilliance. Talk about life-changing!

Here's a remarkable truth: One moment in God's presence is more powerful than years of trying to figure things out on your own. One hour of praise and worship—truly seeking the Lord—can radically shift your heart and reawaken your spirit.

It happened for Sadie and for Isaiah. It can happen for you. Want rest for your soul? Get into God's presence.

I just want to be where You are, Lord Jesus! Amen.

Seek God, Seek His Presence

Seek the LORD and his strength; seek his presence continually!
1 CHRONICLES 16:11 ESV

Some people say, "Seek God, not His presence." Is that wise advice, in light of today's scripture?

We certainly should draw near to God and pursue a strong relationship with Him. Yes, it's about the Person, not the experience. But with our amazing Creator, there's always a package deal. When you get Him, you get His presence too. And that's where the power is. The peace. The motivation to move forward.

Moses spoke directly with God yet still asked to *see* His glory (Exodus 33:18). This man of faith knew something that we often forget—one moment in God's presence brings all the power we need to get through any of our worldly troubles.

Think about it this way: You want to hang out with your best friend. Why? Because you enjoy her company. You come away from your time together feeling better about life. You're encouraged and grateful you have someone to share your heart with.

Amplify those feelings a million times to understand what you get when you seek God and His presence.

I want to be near You, Jesus. I love You and I love Your presence! You give me all I need, and I'm so grateful! Amen.

Guided into Truth

"When the Spirit of truth comes, he will guide you into all the truth, for he will not speak on his own authority, but whatever he hears he will speak, and he will declare to you the things that are to come."

JOHN 16:13 ESV

Imagine you go out for a solitary hike in the wilderness. You soon find yourself in unfamiliar territory, far off the trail, surrounded by thick forest. The sun is hidden, you can't get your bearings, and you don't know which way to turn. Panic begins to grip you as you blunder ahead, getting even more lost than you were before.

That's what it's like when we set out on our own without Jesus. We're wandering blindly in unfamiliar territory, unable to get our bearings. Darkness creeps in, and we become even more afraid.

But when Jesus' light shines through, when we're able to see clearly again, everything suddenly makes sense. We find our way back to the path. . .His path.

You were always meant to walk in the light. If you're feeling lost and overwhelmed, weary and frazzled, maybe it's because you're off the beaten path. Time to get back on the trail! Listen for the Lord's still, small voice. He's always been right there with you.

Lord, thank You for sticking with me. I'm so grateful I'm never really lost because You're closer than my next breath. Amen.

The Way You Should Go

This is what the LORD, who saves you, the Holy One of Israel, says: "I am the LORD your God, who teaches you to do what is good, who leads you in the way you should go."
ISAIAH 48:17 NCV

You've had a lot of great teachers over the years—in school, on the job, even in life. (Think of those women who taught you how to cook and tend things around the home.) You've had some great Bible teachers too—everyone from pastors to small group leaders to friends with deep spiritual roots. You've been blessed to be surrounded by such wise guides.

When it comes to spiritual guidance, though, you can't get any better than the Lord Himself. He will lead you in the way you should go. No one else can say that with honesty. They could say, "I'll lead you in a good direction," or "I'll lead you in the way *I* think you should go." But no one but God can definitively claim, "I'm leading you in the *exact right way*." No one but God can know His own perfect will for your life.

He knows the way, and He's happy to lead you in it. So let Him be your teacher, friend, and guide. You won't be sorry!

Thank You for knowing where I'm headed, Lord, and for guiding me there. I'm safe with You. Amen.

Trust in Him

You keep him in perfect peace whose mind is stayed on you, because he trusts in you.
ISAIAH 26:3 ESV

Nelly had a hard time trusting. After a tumultuous relationship with her first husband—a cheater—she found it difficult to believe in any man. Then a rough situation at the office hurt her confidence in the workplace too. Nelly reached a point where nothing felt trustworthy. She began to doubt everything and everyone. Was anything what it purported to be? Was everyone bound to let her down in the end?

Maybe you can relate. You've been hurt. You're wondering who you can trust.

Here's the truth: If you look to anything on this earth—man, woman, institution—you'll be disappointed. Human beings will let you down. They'll go back on promises, talk about you behind your back, betray you at the drop of a hat. They're human, after all, and humans are broken by sin.

But God? He'll never do any of those things. You can safely place your full trust in Him. When He says, "Trust in Me," you can. Give it a try and see if you don't sense that perfect peace.

Today I choose to place my trust in You, Jesus. I know You won't let me down! Amen.

Don't Lean on Your Own Understanding

Trust in the LORD *with all your heart,*
and do not lean on your own understanding.

PROVERBS 3:5 ESV

Ever leaned a ladder against a wall and then started climbing? Here's a simple and obvious truth: That ladder is only as safe as the wall it leans against. Put it up to a weak, damaged wall and you're going to end up tumbling to the floor.

Leaning on our own understanding is kind of like putting a ladder against an unstable wall. It's not safe. It's not secure. We're eventually going to come tumbling down.

When we lean against the Lord, though? There's no risk of falling. He is steady and secure. He doesn't change His mind every day or two. He doesn't have hidden motivations. He's the wisest of the wise, the only one who truly has answers for the problems you're facing.

Stop trying to figure things out on your own. Go to Jesus. Lean on Him. You can trust His thoughts, even when you can't trust your own.

I'll lean the ladder of my life against You, Lord! With You, I'm safe. I give You my whole heart, as well as my trust. Amen.

Make the Lord Your Trust

How happy is the man who has made the Lord his trust, and has not turned to the proud or to the followers of lies.
PSALM 40:4 NLV

Sometimes shady people have a winning smile and convincing tone of voice. The stereotype is the used-car salesman saying, "You can trust me, folks!" Then two months later the car breaks down and he's nowhere to be found.

Not everyone who claims to be trustworthy actually is. There are certainly a lot of scam artists out there. But you can place your trust in the Lord and be absolutely sure that He's worthy of it.

Don't follow after liars—you've seen their tricks, and you don't want to get caught in their trap. Don't follow after the prideful—they're bound to tumble at some point. Place your full trust in the only one who is worthy. When you do, happiness will follow. Yes, "*happy* is the man who has made the Lord his trust."

Have you done that yet? If not, this is the perfect day!

I place my trust in You and no other, Lord. You're the only one worthy of my praise and my trust! Amen.

Don't Trust What Is Empty

"Let him not lie to himself and trust in what is empty. For what is empty will be his reward."
JOB 15:31 NLV

Job's friends got a lot of things wrong. But sometimes they swerved into truth too. Like Eliphaz did in today's scripture.

Many people put trust in things like their job or their bank account or their stuff. They think too highly of those things, believing them more important than they really are. These folks forget that *God* is the source of life, not the stuff He's blessed them with.

Deep down, we all know we can't take those things with us when we die. They're empty shells, of no real value from an eternal perspective. The words of Eliphaz are true—that bank account will mean nothing when you're standing at the gates of heaven. If your goal on earth is fame and fortune, your reward will be emptiness.

So don't lie to yourself. Don't trust in silly things. Go for the solid reward of your solid Rock, Jesus Christ.

I've done it, Lord. I've put my trust in the things of this earth. But they are not my source—You are! May I never forget that. Amen.

We Are like Him

And so we know and rely on the love God has for us. God is love. Whoever lives in love lives in God, and God in them. This is how love is made complete among us so that we will have confidence on the day of judgment: In this world we are like Jesus.

1 John 4:16–17 niv

Sometimes, in a litter of puppies, there's one that just looks different from the others. Maybe in a group of black pups there's a spotted one. Or one of the babies is much smaller than its mates. Or it just doesn't resemble its mother at all.

How about you? Is it obvious where you're from?

God wants you to resemble Him. Nobody should ever say, "Huh, she doesn't look like she belongs to Him." We clearly belong to God when we love like He does.

We love others when they're angry. We love them when they're confused. We love them when they insist there is no God. We love them when they're lost and don't know which way to turn.

Be Jesus to them. Let the love of God so reign in your heart that others are drawn to you and ultimately to Him.

Thank You, Jesus, for pouring out Your love in my heart! I want to love others as You love them. Help me, I pray. Amen.

Ponder in Your Heart

Be angry, and do not sin; ponder in your own hearts on your beds, and be silent.
Psalm 4:4 ESV

Luke 2:19 also uses the word *ponder* that we find in today's scripture. In the Gospel account, the angel Gabriel has just told Mary that she's about to become pregnant with the Savior. And she "treasured up all these things, pondering them in her heart" (ESV).

How do you keep information like that inside? Let's face it—most women would rather share the news! But Mary somehow kept the shocking truth inside rather than shouting it to the masses.

How about you? Do you ponder things in your heart? Today's scripture indicates it's a good thing to do when you're worked up—say when you've had it with a child or a coworker or a friend. Don't spout off and give them a piece of your mind. That won't bring peace. Instead, be silent. Give it some thought. *Give it to Jesus.* In the end, He'll take care of everything.

Sometimes I want to spout off, Lord. But You say I'd do better to ponder things in my heart. Hold my tongue, please, unless I'm praying to You. Amen.

Discouraged over Failures

Now, however, you should forgive him and encourage him, in order to keep him from becoming so sad as to give up completely.
2 Corinthians 2:7 GNT

None of us like to point the finger at ourselves. When we're going through a rough season, when things aren't going our way, the very last person we want to blame is me, myself, or I. If we're honest, though, there are plenty of times when we ourselves have caused the problem.

Think back to the last big trial you faced. Was there anything you could have done differently? If you had said a certain thing or made a certain move, would the outcome have been changed for the better? If your attitude had been slightly improved, would that have made a difference in how things ended? Very possibly so.

Now, though, be ready to forgive yourself. Yes, you did some things wrong. Sure, they caused a few bumps in the road. But there's still plenty of road ahead. Don't let discouragement over your mistakes slow you down. Confess, receive your forgiveness, and keep moving forward.

I make a lot of mistakes, Jesus, and I get disappointed in myself. But You forgive and forget when I confess. Now please help me to move forward. Amen.

Where the Glory Streams Down

Here I am depressed and downcast. Yet I will still remember you as I ponder the place where your glory streams down from the mighty mountaintops, lofty and majestic—the mountains of your awesome presence.

Psalm 42:6 TPT

Jill was having a terrible day when she decided to get out of the house and go for a drive. Since she lived near the coast, she made her way to the water. Sometimes the waves lifted her spirits.

She pulled up to her favorite beach and got out for a long walk. There, with the wind and waves doing their thing, Jill found herself centered again. The troubles of the day seemed to roll out with each new wave.

Think of today's scripture in light of Jill's experience. There she was—depressed and downcast. Yet as she spent time in nature, taking in the glorious ocean and pondering God's greatness, her thinking changed.

The Creator is bigger than your circumstances. He's bigger than the entire universe! Sometimes we just need a reminder. If you're struggling, take a drive to a lake or a mountain or a beach. If you can't get away like that, simply stare up into the sky. Contemplate the vastness of your God. If He could create everything, He can surely take care of you!

You're an awesome God, Creator of all.
I know I can trust You with my life. Amen.

How Quickly We Forget!

I remember the days of old; I meditate on all that you have done; I ponder the work of your hands.
PSALM 143:5 ESV

You know how it is: God does something marvelous for you and you celebrate. You can't get over how He came through for you, and in the eleventh hour, no less! You're sure you'll never forget His goodness.

But you do. A couple of weeks later you're facing a completely different crisis. Instead of recalling what He did last time, you panic. You can't seem to remember His faithfulness or His goodness. Fear kicks in and you stray, step by step, away from God.

How do you suppose that makes Him feel? He's such a good Father, and He's taken care of you a thousand times over. He was there to make sure your rent was paid. He took care of that health crisis. He even came through for you when your car was on the blink. What makes you think He can't handle crisis number 4,937? He can, girl. And He will.

Remember what God has done in the past. As you ponder the former things, He'll give you courage for the present things. That's how it works!

I won't forget the former things, Lord. How could I, when You came through for me in such magnificent ways? I'll stick with You—today, tomorrow, and always. Amen.

God's Abilities Rise to the Top

Great are the works of the LORD; they are pondered by all who delight in them.
PSALM 111:2 NIV

You're watching a quiz show on TV. One contestant is clearly better than the others. In fact, he's light-years beyond the rest. You know without a shadow of a doubt that he'll win—and win big.

In this game of life, God is the clear winner. He's the only one with the goods. Think about that: There are a lot of talented, intelligent people who can do amazing things—doctors, scientists, artists, philanthropists. They've got skills, and lots of them. But God? His abilities supersede all of them! He can do vastly more than any human being could even consider. His knowledge, His wisdom, His power, and His goodness are, in fact, limitless.

Once you see God in the proper light, it's easier to put your trust in Him. How amazing are His deeds! Think on these things.

Your abilities go above and beyond, God! You're the one with the goods. No matter how many amazing people I meet in this life, I'll never meet anyone who even comes close to You! Amen.

Taste and See

Oh, taste and see that the LORD is good!
Blessed is the man who takes refuge in him!
PSALM 34:8 ESV

"How do you know you don't like it unless you try it?" Your mom probably said something like that as you stared at a plate of brussels sprouts or spinach. And you replied, "I don't have to try it, Mom. I can just tell."

Though that's not entirely true, of course. Until you actually do try something, you really don't know. Don't you eat a lot of things now that you wouldn't go near as a child?

Our relationship with Jesus operates in a similar way. Until you actually "taste and see" that He is good, you don't really know. Oh, others can tell you He's good, and you want to believe it. But deep down you wonder if He'll someday fail you like everyone else has done.

He won't. And as you taste and see His goodness, you begin to relax. You settle in. You place your trust—in Him, in His plan, in His timing.

What's not happening? You're not stressing out. You're able to rest—genuinely. Doesn't it feel good to trust Jesus?

I trust You, Jesus! I've tasted and seen that You are good!
And I'm so grateful for Your love and care. Amen.

He's So Good!

Oh, thank God—he's so good! His love never runs out. All of you set free by God, tell the world! Tell how he freed you from oppression, then rounded you up from all over the place, from the four winds, from the seven seas.

Psalm 107:1–3 msg

Some days you'll question the goodness of God. Barb was in one of those times. Her mother was hospitalized with pneumonia on the same day her own daughter stopped speaking to her over political differences. How unfair! How could a good God allow Mom to suffer? And how could He allow her daughter to overreact like that? Stuck in the middle, Barb was wishing for a way out.

No doubt you've felt that way at times. There are seasons of life when everything happening around you feels wholly unfair. You're upset and angry and feeling justified in your disrespectful response to the Lord.

Remember, dear friend. . .He's still good. Even when everything else is bad, He is good. In our broken, fallen world, horrific things happen to wonderful, godly people. Because He loves us, His heart is broken too. So instead of turning against Him, remind yourself of scriptures like today's. The Lord is good, even when the news is bad.

I'm grateful for Your goodness, Father! I don't always feel it, but I refuse to believe You're anything but good. Please help me through the bad times of this life. Amen.

Drink Deeply

Drink deeply of the pleasures of this God. Experience for yourself the joyous mercies he gives to all who turn to hide themselves in him.
PSALM 34:8 TPT

Read "drink deeply of the pleasures of this God," and what comes to mind? Do you see yourself on a tropical island, feet up, enjoying the sound of the crashing waves? Maybe you think of a stirring worship service, where your hands are lifted in praise. Or maybe you're there in the holy of holies—just you and Jesus—enjoying His presence.

Chances are good this verse doesn't bring to mind the hard seasons of life. But it should.

Sometimes you have to seek the pleasures of God in the very midst of a storm. When you're lying in a hospital bed. When you're facing a financial crisis. When you're not sure how you're going to handle another day with that crazy boss of yours.

But even then you can drink deeply of all that God has for you. In fact, that's the very best time for it! You can experience for yourself the joyous mercies He pours out. They're especially tasty in troubled times.

I'll come to You, Jesus, even when everything around me seems to be falling apart. Thank You for those mercies, Lord! Amen.

The Buffet Table

When I look at you, I see how you have taken my fruit and tasted my word. Your life has become clean and pure, like a lamb washed and newly shorn. You now show grace and balance with truth on display.

Song of Solomon 4:2 TPT

Imagine you're at a buffet and everything looks good. Your eyes are drawn this way and that, so you don't even know where to begin. In the end, of course, you take a little of everything.

Walking with Jesus is something like that. Everything on the table is good—perfect, in fact. He has so many amazing offerings for you that it's hard to know where to begin. He's given you His Word, His Spirit, and the promise of eternity with Him. He's given you life and health and relationships worth pursuing. He's promised to walk with you in good seasons and bad and to carry your burdens for you.

Whew, that's quite the buffet. So grab the biggest plate you can find. Make your way to the table and dish up big portions! You'll rest easy when your plate is full of His goodness.

I'll come to You, Jesus. I've sampled and seen that everything on Your table is the best! Thanks for Your willingness to bless me with all You have and are. Amen.

The Lord, Our Protector

The Lord *is good; he protects his people in times of trouble; he takes care of those who turn to him.*

Nahum 1:7 GNT

Have you ever sensed God's protection over your life? Maybe you've been in an accident but came away unhurt. Or perhaps you came close to having an accident but He intervened. There's no telling how many thousands of times God has swept in and saved us from calamity.

Today's scripture is a lovely reminder that your heavenly Father protects you in times of trouble. You might be thinking, *Really? What about that time (fill in the blank)?* But you're still here, right now, reading this book.

Here's the thing: We were never promised a life free of trouble. But Nahum 1:7 is an assurance that, if you turn to God, He will take care of you. No matter what you're facing today—good or bad, happy or sad—turn toward Him. He's right there, and He's so, so good!

I can't even imagine how many times You've intervened in my life, Lord. Even during the hardest of seasons, You were right there. I'm so grateful. I can rest easy in Your protective arms. Amen.

He Is Enough

My flesh and my heart may fail, but God is the strength of my heart and my portion forever.
PSALM 73:26 NIV

"I feel like something is missing from my life." Debra's nose wrinkled as she uttered the words. "I can't quite put my finger on it, but something's not quite there yet."

"What do you mean?" her friend asked.

Debra shrugged. "I'm just in wait-and-see mode. On a husband. On the right job. On the right place to live."

"Ah, I see." Melissa gave Debra a pensive look. "Did it ever occur to you that maybe *nothing* is missing? That this season might be exactly what it is for a purpose? Don't get so caught up in what you think is missing that you overlook all the blessings you *do* have."

When we're in that wait-and-see mode, it's easy to feel as if where we are—and what we have—isn't enough.

But God is enough. No matter what you're feeling, He's the strength of your heart and your portion forever. He's enough in every season—lean or plentiful. In fact, He's more than enough to see you through.

I get it, Jesus. Help me to stop focusing on what's missing in my life. You've blessed me abundantly! In spite of my feelings, thank You for being enough. Amen.

When I Am Weak. . .He Is Strong

But he answered me, "My grace is always more than enough for you, and my power finds its full expression through your weakness." So I will celebrate my weaknesses, for when I'm weak I sense more deeply the mighty power of Christ living in me.

2 CORINTHIANS 12:9 TPT

"Celebrate my weaknesses? Is that really something God expects of me?"

Today's scripture may raise questions like that. And yet, the idea is tucked away in the middle of the text: "I will celebrate my weaknesses, for when I'm weak I sense more deeply the mighty power of Christ living in me."

When we are weak, *He* is strong. When we can't, He can. When we're done, He's just getting started.

What are your greatest weaknesses? Fear? Jealousy? Pain? Whatever issue you're battling today, that's the very place where God can show off. And remember. . .if you're just not feeling it, He has grace enough to carry you through. The power God brings to a situation finds its full expression through your weakness. So don't ever apologize for being weak. That's the key to God's entrance!

I don't always like admitting I'm weak, Lord. But I trust You to do what I cannot. When I am weak, You are strong! Amen.

The All-Sufficient Cross

For the Anointed One has sent me on a mission, not to see how many I could baptize, but to proclaim the good news. And I declare this message stripped of all philosophical arguments that empty the cross of its true power. For I trust in the all-sufficient cross of Christ alone.

1 Corinthians 1:17 TPT

Maybe you've heard of believers who lean heavily on their own good works. They have a long list of dos and don'ts and try not to deviate from it.

Don't go there.

The cross was enough. God knew you couldn't keep up with all kinds of rules and regulations. The Old Testament covenant proved that—people kept messing up. So the Father sent His Son, Jesus, to be the once-and-for-all answer to sin.

Think about dieting. So often the more we limit certain foods, the more we crave them. Works-based religion is similar. The more you avoid certain things, the more tempting they become.

God wants you to live a good life, a safe life, a healthy life that blesses Him. And He wants your thoughts and actions to be as pure as possible. But He knows you're not perfect—no one is. So give yourself some grace. The cross was enough.

I'll do my best to live according to Your principles, Lord. But when I mess up—and I know I will—I'll give myself some grace. Thank You for the all-sufficient cross! Amen.

Sufficient for the Day

"Therefore do not be anxious about tomorrow, for tomorrow will be anxious for itself. Sufficient for the day is its own trouble."
MATTHEW 6:34 ESV

What keeps you up at night? Specifically, what keeps you from falling asleep? What are you worried about?

Chances are good you're fretting over tomorrow. At times we all do. We don't know what lives there. We can't see it, so we speculate, getting caught up in the what-ifs. We picture all sorts of possibilities, none of them good. The human mind always seems to go straight to the worst scenario.

Tomorrow will reveal itself soon enough. But right now, today, you can't let it consume you.

Reread today's scripture. Jesus was very specific that His followers should not be anxious about tomorrow. When we worry about the unseen, we're taking our eyes off the only one who can actually see into tomorrow! Jesus knows what's coming and He's not worried—so why should we be?

Today has its own struggles. Go ahead and get through those, then face tomorrow when it comes. Many of the things we worry about never actually come to pass anyway.

I give my tomorrows to You, Lord. And I'll rest easy as I place my trust in Your goodness and mercy. Amen.

Generous to a Fault

Generous to a fault, you lavish your favor on all creatures.
Psalm 145:16 MSG

Have you ever met someone who's generous to a fault? Some would say that the overly generous person gives too much, often at her own expense.

Now think of that in terms of what God did for us. He gave. . .at His own expense. He was generous to a fault when He sent His Son to redeem us from our sins and to buy us back from the grave. He lavished favor, peace, joy, and rest. And He poured out eternity as an offering, trickling down from the hands and feet of a broken Savior.

The next time you question whether God is enough—whether His way is really *the* way—remember this verse. He was (and is) generous with you in a thousand different ways. And all He asks in return is your heart. Are you ready to give it to Him? Oh, friend, if you haven't already done so, this is the perfect opportunity to give your heart, mind, and soul to the God who loves you dearly. He will give you eternity, beginning right now!

Lord, I thank You that eternity can begin right now, in my broken heart. Take it, mend it, and fill it with Yourself, I pray. I accept Your gift of salvation, Jesus. Thank You for Your generosity as You pour out Your life for me. Amen.

Good News!

Therefore, since the promise of entering his rest still stands, let us be careful that none of you be found to have fallen short of it. For we also have had the good news proclaimed to us, just as they did; but the message they heard was of no value to them, because they did not share the faith of those who obeyed.

HEBREWS 4:1–2 NIV

You know the joy of good news. Maybe you learned that a baby was on the way. Or perhaps you were told of an unexpected raise at work. Good news is, well, *good*! It leaves you feeling like you could walk on air.

God shared the best news of all through Jesus. That news? "I love you so much that I'm willing to give My all for you!" Not just anyone would do that. But His love runs so deep, so wide, so high and long that it extended all the way from heaven to earth. . .and then back again. Because of God's great love, we have access to His kingdom.

Now that's good news!

So what are you going to do with it? Receive it for yourself and spread that message far and wide. May your life be a walking, talking example of God's love for everyone.

Lord, I'm so grateful for the good news of the gospel. You truly gave Your all. How can I ever begin to thank You? I'll live every day trying. Amen.

Until the Whole World Knows

"And this gospel of the kingdom will be preached in the whole world as a testimony to all nations, and then the end will come."
MATTHEW 24:14 NIV

The gospel will be preached in the whole world. Fifty years ago we might have asked ourselves, "How? How in the world can the whole world be reached?"

Incredible advances in technology make it easier to imagine how an entire planet could receive the gospel message. And who knows what the engineers and inventors have yet to come up with!

This message will go forth as a testimony, and your little part of it—your own story—is part of the whole. Don't take your part lightly. You're one piece in a giant puzzle, but puzzles are incomplete without every last piece.

So stick with God. Let Him love you through the rough patches. When you're in a low place, remember that the puzzle is being assembled, one piece at a time. Allow God to use your testimony to minister to others in need. How marvelous to be included in His story!

Use me to reach the world, Jesus! I don't know what that looks like, but I'm ready and willing to spread Your love to the lost. Guide me, I pray. Amen.

The Best News Ever!

For I am not ashamed of the gospel, for it is the power of God for salvation to everyone who believes, to the Jew first and also to the Greek.

ROMANS 1:16 ESV

Imagine you're leaving the doctor's office. You've been waiting for days for test results, and the news has just arrived. You do not have cancer! It's the best news ever.

What are you thinking now? What are you feeling? Who do you call first?

That same sense of joy should drive your life as you contemplate the good news of salvation. Your life has been spared! Your pain has been taken away by someone else, the Son of God who offered Himself on your behalf.

What happened on the cross was the most excellent thing ever to happen to humanity. It's worth picking up the phone! It's worth a celebration! And it leads to rest for your soul. When the news is good, you can truly rest easy.

Still need convincing? If Jesus cared enough to go to the cross for you, don't you think He cares enough to bring you through the trials of this life? Of course He does!

The message of the cross is truly the best news ever, Jesus. How can I ever begin to thank You for what You've done? I'm forever grateful! Amen.

Good News of Great Joy

And the angel said to them, "Fear not, for behold, I bring you good news of great joy that will be for all the people."
LUKE 2:10 ESV

Think of those shepherds outside Bethlehem on the first Christmas night. An angel appeared to them, saying, "Fear not, for behold, I bring you *good news*"! This was no somber announcement or some kind of celestial chastisement. It was good, even excellent, news!

According to the angel, the good news was that great joy was coming for all people. Not some of the people. Not a select group, but everyone. Including you.

You can rest easy in this good news. Don't let the cares of life drag you down. Sure, you'll get some bad news—sometimes very bad news—at times. But there's a much greater message, proclaimed by the heavens, that joy can be yours. And if you know Jesus, the joy is already yours.

Good news of great joy, Jesus! That's what You bring to every situation in my life. I am forever changed by Your love. Amen.

Go into All the World

Declare his glory among the nations,
his marvelous deeds among all peoples.
Psalm 96:3 NIV

Not that long ago, you had to become a foreign missionary to take God's Word to the world. These days it's a simple matter of sharing your testimony on social media. Your words can impact the world in a millisecond. You can lift the spirits of a woman in Zimbabwe. You can encourage a family in India. You can change the thinking of a person at a crossroads anywhere.

You have good news to share, and it could very well bring rest to a lot of troubled souls. But how will they know if you don't tell them? How will they experience hope if you don't share that Jesus is the hope giver?

You have excellent news on the tip of your tongue. . .or at the tips of your fingers. Might as well put it out there, girl!

I'm grateful to live in the internet age, Lord, when I can share my day-to-day testimony on social media. Show me how best to reach others with Your love. Amen.

A Spirit at Rest

My spirit was not at rest because I did not find my brother Titus there. So I took leave of them and went on to Macedonia. But thanks be to God, who in Christ always leads us in triumphal procession, and through us spreads the fragrance of the knowledge of him everywhere.
2 CORINTHIANS 2:13–14 ESV

At times everything around you seems okay. But deep in your gut, you're troubled. Something is amiss.

There will be days when you feel totally at peace. Then there will be other days when you're struggling and can't quite put your finger on why. On those days, ask God to calm your spirit, and trust that He can handle the things you can't figure out on your own. Even the deep, hidden things. (He's really good at rooting those out, by the way.)

What's troubling you today? Whatever it is, know that God can lead you through it in triumphal procession. That is, He's not going to drag you over the finish line—you're going to march in the victory parade! Shouldn't that bring peace to your spirit?

Thank You for leading me through, Lord! When I feel troubled, You know how to calm me down. I can't always put my finger on why I feel off, but You know. . .and You bring peace to my spirit. I'm grateful! Amen.

How Great the Love of God!

Dear friends, let us love one another, for love comes from God. Everyone who loves has been born of God and knows God. Whoever does not love does not know God, because God is love.

1 John 4:7–8 niv

Do you ever ponder the love of God? It's deeper than the ocean, higher than the tallest mountain, stronger than a hurricane, and more intense than the love of the most passionate husband and wife. God is quite enthusiastic about *you*!

Contemplating His great love can make the trials you're going through more manageable. Think of the times you've walked through a rough season with your husband or a close friend. God's vast love dwarfs even our best human relationships.

In fact, His love boggles the mind. Though all God saw on earth was rebellion and sin, He chose to send His Son to die on a cross to provide forgiveness for anyone who'd take it. Jesus didn't have to come to earth for us, but He chose to do so out of His great love. Rest easy in that amazing love today.

My soul is at rest because of Your great love, Lord! Amen.

Be Like Jesus

We know that we are children of God, and that the whole world is under the control of the evil one. We know also that the Son of God has come and has given us understanding, so that we may know him who is true. And we are in him who is true by being in his Son Jesus Christ. He is the true God and eternal life.

1 John 5:19–20 NIV

"The whole world is under the control of the evil one."

Well, that's an intimidating thought. If you knew that your home was under the spell of some evil force, would you want to live there? Probably not.

But here's the best news of all—God is greater than Satan. Our Lord is far greater than any force of darkness. And He's placed us here—in this world that's under the control of the evil one—knowing we can not only survive but make an impact.

Jesus' teaching and example show how to do that. So follow His lead. Stay dedicated to God. Remain true to the calling He has placed on your life. Hang with like-minded people, just as Jesus Himself did with His disciples. Love people. Pray for your enemies. And always point yourself toward heaven, keeping an eternal perspective.

Be like Jesus. He is the true God and eternal life.

I want to be more like You, Jesus! Whenever I stray, draw me back. I want to stand strong against the powers of the enemy, able to make a difference in this broken world. Amen.

This Present Age

For the grace of God has appeared that offers salvation to all people. It teaches us to say "No" to ungodliness and worldly passions, and to live self-controlled, upright and godly lives in this present age, while we wait for the blessed hope—the appearing of the glory of our great God and Savior, Jesus Christ, who gave himself for us to redeem us from all wickedness and to purify for himself a people that are his very own, eager to do what is good.

TITUS 2:11–14 NIV

Do you ever wish you'd been born in a different age? You know, when things were easier?

Then again, were things ever *easier*? A hundred years ago there were no dishwashers, microwaves, or cell phones. Life's been tough in every age of human history.

But God put you right here, right now for a reason. He knew you had the ability to impact your world. He's given you the desire, the wisdom, and the power to make a difference—by living an upright, self-controlled, godly life in front of others. Then they can come to know Him too.

Let's face it—every era has had its woes. But every person in every era was born right then for God's purposes. He knows what He's doing.

I was born for this age, Lord. Help me to represent You well to a lost and broken human race. Amen.

Sometimes Things Get Weird

*"Though the mountains be shaken and the hills be removed,
yet my unfailing love for you will not be shaken nor my covenant
of peace be removed," says the Lord, who has compassion on you.*

Isaiah 54:10 NIV

Have you ever been through a break-up? It can be brutal. Whether you're breaking it off with a boyfriend or your husband—or even just ending a friendship—those "severings" can knock the wind out of your sails.

Once that relationship is a thing of the past, things are weird. You don't speak. You avoid each other at social functions. It's just. . .awkward.

Happily, things with God never get weird. He's never going to break up with you. It doesn't matter what you do or don't do—He'll be there with and for you.

You'll fail Him time and time again, but He won't let you go. You're worth the trouble to Him. In fact, He would go a step further and say that you were worth a trip to the cross.

If things between you and God ever do feel weird, think about this: It's not Him. That means it must be you!

*I get it, Lord. I don't need to lose sleep thinking You'll
dump me. We're in this relationship for all eternity!
Thanks for loving me so much. Amen.*

The Power of the Spirit

May the God of hope fill you with all joy and peace in believing, so that by the power of the Holy Spirit you may abound in hope.
ROMANS 15:13 ESV

Imagine a battery-operated toy dog. When his batteries are fresh, he's on the go, moving across the room, doing backflips, yap-yap-yapping. But as his batteries wear down, he s-l-o-w-s down. He can't flip. He can't bark. He can barely move.

Ever felt that way yourself?

You've reached the "depleted" stage more often than you'd like to admit. And when you do, nothing seems possible. You're like that little pup, dragging his feet in slow motion.

That's when you need the power of the Holy Spirit, sister! When He fills you up, you get megadoses of joy, peace, and hope. And those things come with the best gift of all—power from on high. It's like plugging yourself into a supercharged outlet, one that jolts you back to life.

Whatever has depleted you today, there is hope. Know that God is standing nearby, ready to pour Himself out on your behalf.

I need Your power, Lord. Nothing else charges my batteries like You do! I've got miles to walk, backflips to do, and people to reach. Jolt me back to life, I pray. Amen.

Fine Stallions on the Run

"Led by the LORD, they were as sure-footed as wild horses, and never stumbled. As cattle are led into a fertile valley, so the LORD gave his people rest. He led his people and brought honor to his name."
ISAIAH 63:13–14 GNT

Have you ever watched horses run? They are pure delight, flying like the breeze, almost without effort.

When the Israelites trekked across the desert, they were feeling more like buffalo than stallions. But then the Spirit of God did something magnificent for them. He sent a sacred gift—rest. And once they received this supernatural rest, the Israelites were "sure-footed as wild horses, and never stumbled."

Maybe you're bogged down in the desert sand today. You're weary and ready to give up. Oh, friend, don't quit! Instead, go straight to your source: God. He will pour out His Spirit and give you everything you need. And God doesn't just drag your feet through the hot sand; He'll enable you to run through the desert, never stumbling. That's some promise.

With God, all things are possible. So start running!

I'm ready to take off running, Lord. Send Your Spirit, I pray. Amen.

Controlled by the Spirit

To be controlled by human nature results in death; to be controlled by the Spirit results in life and peace.
ROMANS 8:6 GNT

"Controlled by the Spirit" equals "life and peace." Now that's a guarantee, isn't it?

When you allow the Spirit of God to take charge of your life, you won't feel manipulated. His "strings" bring peace. . .life. . .joy. . . contentment. Cut those strings and pursue the world's ways and you'll pay a heavy price. You'll find yourself burdened with cares quicker than you can say, "Oops! Shouldn't have done that!"

So what does it look like to be controlled by the Spirit? Tasha found out at a family reunion where politics prevailed. Half the family took one side of an issue; the others believed the opposite. Out of love for the whole family, she decided to let God's Spirit take control of her tongue.

Oh, there were things she wanted to say, but she didn't. After everyone parted ways, her phone was filled with texts thanking her for applying the salve of peace. The Spirit of God brought rest to a potentially tumultuous situation.

I get it, Lord. I can trust Your Spirit to calm the troubled waters, even in the midst of upheaval. Today I give You the strings of my life. Take charge, Spirit of God! Amen.

A Day Is Like a Thousand Years

Do not overlook this one fact, beloved, that with the Lord one day is as a thousand years, and a thousand years as one day. The Lord is not slow to fulfill his promise as some count slowness, but is patient toward you, not wishing that any should perish, but that all should reach repentance.

2 Peter 3:8–9 ESV

Some days never seem to end. Some seasons are like that too. You start to wonder if you'll ever break through into brighter times.

For the woman of God, there are always brighter times ahead. But you've got to hang on till you get there! Keep your eyes on the Lord, and remember that His timing (like all of His ways) differs from ours. Don't ruin your sleep in the not-so-great seasons, because you'll want all your energy available for the happier one that's coming.

If a day is like a thousand years to the Lord, He must understand our long, tedious seasons. But today's scripture also says a thousand years are like a day to Him. It will be like that for you too. One day—soon enough—you'll look back on this hard season and see just a blip on the radar. You'll barely remember the details or even the pain of it.

I will keep my days in perspective, Lord!
They are all in Your hand! Amen.

Full of Joy. . .No Matter What

This is the day that the Lord has made.
Let us be full of joy and be glad in it.
Psalm 118:24 NLV

You'll have good days and bad days. Some days you'll feel like throwing a party. Others? Not at all. You'll wish you could stay in bed with the covers pulled up to your chin.

With that truth in mind, can you keep your days in perspective? The good ones and the bad? Can you keep your emotions from swinging back and forth by acknowledging that everyone—rich or poor, young or old—faces the same ups and downs?

Seek God. Focus on Him. He'll help you with the perspective you need. And on those days when things are rough, when you're absolutely sure you'll never be happy again, He'll give you the strength to turn your attitude around. He'll help you to be full of joy and rejoice in your day, whatever sort it is.

God is the giver of abundant life. He's worthy of your praise, on good days and bad.

I'll praise You today, Lord, even when I'm not feeling it.
I'll do my best to keep things in perspective. Amen.

Shepherds Watching over Their Flocks

"Thus says the Lord *of hosts: In this place that is waste, without man or beast, and in all of its cities, there shall again be habitations of shepherds resting their flocks."*
Jeremiah 33:12 ESV

Think about sheep in the field. Do they spend their days fretting over what they'll eat, where they'll live, or who will protect them from the big, bad wolf? No. They rest easy, grazing on green grass and simply trusting their shepherd. How do they know he's trustworthy? Because he's never let them down.

And God has never let *you* down. Oh, you've been through some rough patches. You've wondered if you would make it. But in the end, He always came through for you. He always led you into a green pasture again, making sure you had everything you needed for life and health.

Reread today's scripture. Don't you love the imagery of "habitations of shepherds resting their flocks"? Can't you just see the good shepherd himself, reclining by his peaceful, rested sheep?

Even now, Jesus is at your side. Your good shepherd is watching over you, tending to your needs, seeking your benefit. Oh, how He cares for you!

Lord, thank You for being my good shepherd, for making sure I have everything I need! I'm so grateful for Your tender loving care. Amen.

Until Then

We are sure of this. We know that while we are at home in this body we are not with the Lord. Our life is lived by faith. We do not live by what we see in front of us. We are sure we will be glad to be free of these bodies. It will be good to be at home with the Lord. So if we stay here on earth or go home to Him, we always want to please Him.

2 CORINTHIANS 5:6–9 NLV

The bodies we have now are temporary. They're frail. Even on the best days, they don't perform at 100 percent, because we live in a fallen world far short of the perfection of heaven.

That said, we look forward to the day when all things are made new, when we'll receive ultimate healing in eternity. Older believers often say, "I'm longing for heaven," but not everyone understands that. If you're not there yet, you will be someday. You'll be ready to trade your rags for riches, the temporary for the eternal, the broken for the whole.

Until then, live by faith. Sure, things here aren't always what you hope. Yes, your body will betray you sometimes. But even on those days, focus your trust on God. Keep speaking words of courage and hope. You'll be emboldened by what comes out of your own mouth.

I'm seeking You, Lord, for this body of mine. It's increasingly tired and broken, but I long for the day when all will be made whole. Until then, I will trust in You. Amen.

A Great Cloud of Witnesses

Therefore, since we are surrounded by such a great cloud of witnesses, let us throw off everything that hinders and the sin that so easily entangles. And let us run with perseverance the race marked out for us, fixing our eyes on Jesus, the pioneer and perfecter of faith. For the joy set before him he endured the cross, scorning its shame, and sat down at the right hand of the throne of God.

HEBREWS 12:1–2 NIV

You're having a bad day. You're not sure you can make it through. You just don't have the energy or the strength.

But think of all the Bible characters who persevered through hard—sometimes incredibly hard—times. There was young David, running for his life from the murderous King Saul. There were Daniel and his three friends, who endured opposition from powerful enemies and survived some very dangerous trials. There was the apostle Paul, who traveled thousands of miles preaching the gospel, along the way experiencing imprisonment, beatings, and shipwreck.

Think how tired they must have been! But at God's urging and in His strength, they kept on. Sure, you're wiped out most days, but you have plenty of biblical cheerleaders urging you forward. They've walked through the fire too—sometimes literally.

Next time you're feeling all alone, remind yourself that you're not. Others have traveled this road before you, and they're watching right now, saying, "Keep going, girl! Don't give up. You've got this. Because God's got *you*!"

I won't give up! I'll follow the lead of those beloved Bible characters, Lord! Amen.

Through the Dark Valley

Even if I walk through a very dark valley, I will not be afraid, because you are with me. Your rod and your shepherd's staff comfort me.
PSALM 23:4 NCV

Deep, dark valleys can be dreary, depressing, even creepy. You lose the sunlight overhead and feel bound by eerie shadows.

Alice went through a valley so deep she wondered if she would ever emerge from it. Her husband, after battling blood cancer for several months, rallied and seemed whole. Then, just as quickly, he plummeted and succumbed to the disease.

Alice's heart was broken and her trust in God badly shaken. But then, in the deepest, darkest valley of her life, the Lord made Himself real to her. She couldn't explain how and when it happened, only that it did. And the shepherd's presence made all the difference. Alice was somehow able to get out of bed, get dressed, and get back to living.

The Lord's rod and staff—tools He uses to protect His sheep and draw them close—bring comfort. There's no need to be afraid. Even when you experience the worst season ever, your shepherd is nearby, guiding and guarding you every step of the way.

Thank You for guiding me, my good shepherd.
The valley is bright when You walk through it with me.
I'm so grateful You've chosen to do that. Amen.

We Are His

Know that the Lord is God. It is he who made us,
and we are his; we are his people, the sheep of his pasture.
Psalm 100:3 NIV

Imagine two shepherds with side-by-side fields. The fence between them blows over in a wind storm. The sheep—which are mostly identical—wander together. They end up in a big jumbled flock.

The shepherds need to sort out their sheep, but how do they know which are which? And how will the sheep know?

According to Jesus, His own sheep "follow him because they know his voice" (John 10:4 NIV). When you hear the still, small voice of your shepherd, you know to follow. You know something else too—you'll be safe in His care.

It's the same with those sheep in the windswept field. They'll eventually make their way back to the right shepherd. Knowing who feeds and cares for them, they want to get home, and the sooner the better.

We can learn some things from sheep.

I want to be home with You, my good shepherd! I know Your voice, Jesus! I hear it often as You speak to my heart. Thank You for loving me into the fold. Amen.

Life Isn't Always Fair

When the Lord has given you rest from your pain and turmoil and the hard service with which you were made to serve, you will take up this taunt against the king of Babylon: "How the oppressor has ceased, the insolent fury ceased!"
Isaiah 14:3–4 ESV

Sometimes we're upset because life just isn't fair. Bad people get away with terrible things. Good people are taken advantage of. Those we love suffer. It stinks!

Jesus understood unfairness. After all, our sinless Savior died a bloody death on a cross so we could have eternal life. That's hardly fair. But He didn't complain. He *chose* the cross to obtain salvation for us—to give us a way out.

And He's still providing ways out. Jesus Himself is pained by the injustices of our world, and He stands by to bring comfort, peace, and healing.

No matter what you're going through, know that God cares. He sees. He will, in His own time and His own way, make things right. And whatever isn't "righted" in this lifetime will be forever and perfectly righted in the next. The best news of all? In eternity none of the things that grieved us here on earth will matter anymore. Our complete focus will be Jesus!

I trust You, Jesus. You paid the price for my sin on the cross. And You are bringing justice to the hard situations I face now—maybe in this lifetime, maybe in eternity. For now, I choose to trust You. Amen.

Payback

God is just: He will pay back trouble to those who trouble you and give relief to you who are troubled, and to us as well. This will happen when the Lord Jesus is revealed from heaven in blazing fire with his powerful angels.

2 THESSALONIANS 1:6–7 NIV

What if we stopped after the first three words of today's scripture? "God is just." He is, absolutely. He always has been and He always will be. Some people say, "That's the God of the Old Testament. The New Testament version isn't like that." Well, this is a New Testament scripture.

Truth is, God wants justice to be done. Because we live in a fallen world, we don't always see true justice. But a day is coming when justice will be served. God will pay back trouble to those who trouble you. And He promises relief to those who are troubled.

Wow—relief to the troubled. How many times have you longed for that? What a day it will be when all the wrongs of this life will be made right. The hot mess of earth will be wiped away, replaced by the cool peace of heaven.

Jesus will be revealed, and all will be made right. Because God is just.

Thank You, my just God! You're going to make everything right. I'll hang on for the ride, knowing that You have a much bigger plan at work here. Amen.

Honest Gain

His sons did not follow his ways. They turned aside after dishonest gain and accepted bribes and perverted justice.
1 Samuel 8:3 niv

If you know the story of Hannah, you know what a miracle it was that she finally gave birth. Her son Samuel grew up to be a godly prophet who impacted Israel in powerful ways.

His kids, though? Reread today's scripture.

When Samuel was older, his sons turned away. They didn't follow their dad's lead, and they certainly didn't chase after the Lord. Instead, they pursued dishonest gain.

What exactly is that? "Dishonest gain" is when you give little (if anything) to get much. It usually takes place to the detriment of someone else. When you're gaining something dishonestly, you're pretty much taking it from someone who deserves it more.

God's no fan of dishonest gain. Commit to honest and honorable dealings in your own business dealings, and don't lose sleep over those who do the wrong thing. In the end, God will deal properly with them. He's just, you know.

Shine Your light on what they're doing, Lord. Convict the dishonest of their sin and bring justice, I pray. Amen.

Joy to the Righteous

When justice is done, it brings joy to the righteous but terror to evildoers.
PROVERBS 21:15 NIV

Sometimes we lose sleep over the unfairness of life. Good people are persecuted. Bad people get away with their evil plans. And your stomach is in knots as you think about it.

Woman of God, you can still rest easy. As awful as injustice is, it's been around since the beginning of time. People turning on people. People lording themselves over others. People persecuting the innocent. It's a horrible, but common, theme.

Take another look at today's scripture. It starts, "When justice is done." Justice *will* be done. A day is coming when God will shine His spotlight on all the evil deeds of this world. He will right the wrongs of this life. That day will bring joy to the righteous. Finally—vindication!

Now see what happens to the evildoers. They're left only with terror. They've been exposed. And once that happens, they have no place to hide.

God will expose both the evil and the good and reward each accordingly. In the meantime, you can trust Him. Justice will be done.

I'll trust You until justice comes to pass, Lord! Whom have I in heaven or on earth but You? Amen.

Learn to Do Good

"Learn to do right. See that justice is done—help those who are oppressed, give orphans their rights, and defend widows."
ISAIAH 1:17 GNT

You might think that "doing good" would come naturally for believers, but this scripture indicates otherwise. We have to *learn* to do good. It's an acquired behavior.

Many, if not most, people in this world are content to live self-centered lives. You, though, are ready and willing to serve. You want to be a blessing—to God and others.

If you wonder how to bring peace to a loved one's heart, be ready to step up. She might just need your physical presence. Or your kind words to get her through a rough patch. She might need your chauffeuring or babysitting or grocery shopping. God brings rest to our own souls as we provide gentle, caring support to the hearts of people in need.

So keep your eyes open, friend. People are hurting. They're feeling overwhelmed. And you might be the very touch of God to bring hope in a hopeless situation.

Thank You for the reminder that I can make a difference in the lives of my friends and loved ones, Jesus. When I see people going through a hard time, use me to bring rest. Amen.

The Bread of Anxious Toil

Unless the LORD builds the house, those who build it labor in vain. Unless the LORD watches over the city, the watchman stays awake in vain. It is in vain that you rise up early and go late to rest, eating the bread of anxious toil; for he gives to his beloved sleep.

PSALM 127:1–2 ESV

You know what it's like. You set a plan in motion and dive in headfirst, ready to conquer your goals. Maybe it's a weight-loss plan. Maybe it's starting a small business. Perhaps it's a women's ministry opportunity you felt led to accept. You take off like a racehorse from the starting gate. But a few months later, you peter out. You just can't anymore. You're done.

Striving does that to us. It wears us out in a hurry! When you "eat the bread of anxious toil," you're basically consuming poison. Anxiety becomes so controlling that even when you finally have an opportunity to rest, you can't. Your stomach is in knots. Your blood pressure is through the roof.

So what's a girl to do? Change the menu. Instead of eating that nasty toil-bread, enjoy some rest-bread instead. Give your goals to God. Ask for His purpose, His way to shine through them. Acknowledge that you don't always know best. Then trust that He has plans for you that go far beyond anything you might have dreamed up.

When you walk in God's way, you don't have to fret. You can rest easy because His plans for you are good. They'll actually invigorate you.

I get it, Jesus. I need Your plans, not my own. Help me to walk in the ones that You've laid out for me—nothing more, nothing less. Amen.

He Blesses Abundantly

And God is able to bless you abundantly, so that in all things at all times, having all that you need, you will abound in every good work.
2 Corinthians 9:8 NIV

When you read, "He blesses abundantly," what comes to mind? Do you picture yourself living in a mansion? Driving a sports car? Taking the yacht out on weekends? Maybe hobnobbing with well-to-do people, attending fancy parties?

God blesses His kids abundantly, but it rarely looks like that stuff. He might bless you by providing the opportunity to minister to a homeless person. Or to purchase groceries for a family in need. Or to bake cookies for an elderly neighbor. God might give you the privilege of serving the children of your church or praying for a friend who's going through a difficult season.

To be honest, God's version of "blessing" looks a lot like service. But that's where the blessings flow—in ministering to others!

Don't lose sleep over the quest to acquire stuff. Lay that down. True peace and rest will come as you pour yourself out for those less fortunate. You'll find yourself as you give yourself away.

I see how this works, Jesus! I want Your blessings, so I'll get busy blessing others! Amen.

Fix Your Thoughts

Finally, brothers and sisters, whatever is true, whatever is noble, whatever is right, whatever is pure, whatever is lovely, whatever is admirable—if anything is excellent or praiseworthy—think about such things.

PHILIPPIANS 4:8 NIV

What are you thinking about right now? What's consuming you? Are you fretting over a bill? Thinking about some person who wronged you? Wondering what you're going to do for lunch? Our thoughts bounce around like a pinball in an arcade game.

Take another look at today's scripture. We're called to think about good things. The New Living Translation says to "fix your thoughts" on these things. That means to hold your thoughts steady, unwavering, on what is good.

Ever heard of people accidentally sticking their fingers to something when applying superglue? It's that kind of "sticking power" that God is commanding. Superglue your thoughts on Him, on His goodness, on His power. Don't give in to the temptation to panic.

What does this have to do with resting your soul in Jesus? Everything! When you're superglued to Him, you don't have time to fret. Your thoughts are firmly affixed to the only thing that matters—your gracious and loving Lord.

I'll superglue my thoughts to You, Jesus! I see You for who You are—my deliverer, healer, provider, and friend. How I praise You for being my all in all! Amen.

All That Remains

As far as the east is from the west, so far does
he remove our transgressions from us.
PSALM 103:12 ESV

Do you realize you have died and risen again, just like Jesus?

As a believer in Jesus, when you truly gave your heart to Him, He took the old you—the one with the shame, the guilt, and the pain—and buried her under the covering of His blood. He hurled your sins as far away as the east is from the west. And as He sent His Spirit to live inside you, you were reborn. Really! The old you is gone. The new you is all that remains.

Read that last sentence again: "The new you is all that remains." So stop looking over your shoulder at where you've been. If those sins have been hurled away, if the old you is gone, the foul vapors of yesterday shouldn't affect today.

Here's a little exercise for you. Stand outside and look to the west. How far can you see? Beyond the sunset? No. Now look to the east. Can you see beyond the sunrise? No. Your vision is limited, but God's is not. He saw yesterday, He sees today, and He already knows tomorrow. And in Christ He's forgiven you, tossing those sins as far as the east is from the west.

Shouldn't that give you a peaceful sleep tonight?

Thank You for Your forgiveness, Lord,
and for second chances. Amen.

Seek Him First

"But seek first the kingdom of God and his righteousness, and all these things will be added to you."
MATTHEW 6:33 ESV

What are you seeking? What do you chase after? For some, it's pleasure, the need to be entertained. For others, it's value, a desire to be known and respected by family, friends, and coworkers. For others, it's health, the quest to stay (or get) in shape and feel better physically.

Some people seek stuff. They want bigger houses, cars, and toys. Others want a high pay grade, so they work tirelessly at the office, hoping to be promoted. Still others seek fame and do all they can to draw attention to themselves.

Many things we seek in this life are good, but here's something to remember—if you chase after Jesus, all the things you really need will come to you. He'll provide shelter. He'll provide income. He'll provide food. He'll provide satisfaction.

The things this world offers? They're nothing but counterfeits. So seek Jesus and His kingdom, and rest in the peace of His provision.

I won't lose sleep over the things I don't have, Lord. Instead, I'll chase after You and trust that You've got me covered in every area of my life. Amen.

If

"If you turn back your foot from the Sabbath, from doing your pleasure on my holy day, and call the Sabbath a delight and the holy day of the LORD honorable; if you honor it, not going your own ways, or seeking your own pleasure, or talking idly; then you shall take delight in the LORD, and I will make you ride on the heights of the earth; I will feed you with the heritage of Jacob your father, for the mouth of the LORD has spoken."

ISAIAH 58:13–14 ESV

If is a teeny-tiny word. But the consequences of these two letters are huge. The "ifs" stir us to action. They keep us walking the straight and narrow. They propel us to do better.

With that in mind, take a closer look at today's scripture: "If you turn back your foot from the Sabbath, from doing your pleasure on my holy day," and "if you honor it, not going your own ways," then the rest of the verse comes into play.

With an *if* there's usually a *then*. Parents, we know how to use the combination: "If you clean your room, then I'll let you watch a show." We say *if* is conditional.

God announced some conditions on His ancient people's Sabbath rest. And though we in New Testament times don't face the same Sabbath rules, we can enjoy similar Sabbath blessings. When we take time for rest and focus on God, good things come to us. We'll "ride on the heights of the earth."

I get it, Lord. If I do what You ask, then You bless me. It's really that simple. Help me do my best. Amen.

The Biggest Word

"If my people who are called by my name will humble themselves and pray and seek my face and turn from their wicked ways, I will hear from heaven and will forgive their sins and restore their land."
2 CHRONICLES 7:14 NLT

We just established that *if* is one of the biggest words in the Bible. A lot hangs on those two tiny letters! Take today's verse, for instance. God says that if His people, who are called by His name, will humble themselves and pray, then. . .what?

Then God will hear from heaven and forgive their sins and restore their land.

Just to be clear: *If* we do our part, *then* He will sweep in and do the impossible. He does what we cannot do. But we have to do some things first. One: humble ourselves. Not an easy thing, as most of us tend to be a bit prideful. Two: pray. Easier, perhaps, but do we do it on a consistent basis? Three: seek His face. We must search out His way, His plan, His purpose. Four: turn from our wicked ways. This is where the rubber meets the road, as some people say.

If we actually do the things God commands, then He will hear from heaven and heal our land. Whatever we put into this effort is completely worth it—there will be rest for ourselves and the people around us.

Lord, what You've asked of me is small compared to what You're willing to do. I'll humble myself and pray and seek Your face. I'll turn from my wicked ways and watch as You bring healing. . .and with it, rest for our souls. Amen.

His Love Is Not Conditional

Dear friends, let us love one another, for love comes from God. Everyone who loves has been born of God and knows God. Whoever does not love does not know God, because God is love.

1 John 4:7–8 niv

You might read these devotions about the word *if* and conclude that God's love is conditional. "If" you live right, "then" He'll love you. Nothing could be further from the truth! God's love is limitless. He'll go right on loving you, no matter how far away from Him you might fall. Sure, some of His *blessings* might have conditions, but His *love* never will. Think about it: If God's love was conditional, why would Jesus die for everyone and not just the good people?

No, Jesus died for sinner and saint alike. And let's face it, none of us are truly saints. So stop beating yourself up every time you make a mistake. Stop saying, "I'm not lovable. How could God possibly love me?" He does, no matter what. There's nothing you could do to change that.

Now, having received such love, we have a job: share God's love with others. Love comes from Him, we pass it on to others, and everyone benefits. Let us continue to love one another.

Lord, I will try to offer Your limitless love to those in my circle. Thank You for not limiting Your love for me. I am truly grateful. Amen.

Hammocked in His Love

And hope does not put us to shame, because God's love has been poured out into our hearts through the Holy Spirit, who has been given to us.
Romans 5:5 NIV

Ever spent time in a hammock? Some are hard to get into. Some are even harder to get out of! But once you're in, that hammock serves as a sort of cocoon. It embraces you. Hugs you. Wraps you up. Keeps you covered.

In many ways, God's love is like that hammock. Sure, you might wrestle your way into it. You might even fight His love at first. But once you're in. . .you're in. You can rest easy in that safe space. He's got you cocooned. Cradled in His arms, where you can safely rest.

This love of God is "poured out into our hearts through the Holy Spirit". . .and what a gift it is. Full of hope, without shame, perfect as our perfect Lord.

Like some hammocks, this love will be impossible to escape from. But why would you want to?

I won't try to wrestle free from Your love, Lord. I've finally found a safe space where I can draw a deep breath and put the chaos of the world behind. Thank You for loving me so beautifully. Amen.

Restored

He restores my soul. He leads me in paths of righteousness for his name's sake.
PSALM 23:3 ESV

Take a close look at the word *restore*. Notice anything interesting? The first four letters are *r-e-s-t*. To be restored, you've got to be rested. Now look at the back end of the word: *store*. When you store something, you put it away for later use. You know right where it is when you need it.

God promises to restore your soul. But first. . .rest your soul. Rest your heart. Rest those crazy thoughts. Only after you've quieted those things can you possibly be restored to fullness of joy. And when that happens, you'll have more than enough.

You might wonder why you've been stuck, why God doesn't seem to be propelling you forward in your job, your ministry, or your relationships. Maybe He's not leading you in paths of righteousness just yet because you haven't accomplished the first part of this verse.

Rest. Be restored.

Then watch as He leads you in the way you should go.

I get it, Lord. . .first, rest. I want to be fully restored so I can be used to my maximum potential. Have Your way in my heart and lead me in the direction I need to go. Amen.

Nothing Is Impossible

"For nothing will be impossible with God."
LUKE 1:37 ESV

Nothing is impossible with God. Nothing you could ever think of is outside the scope of His ability.

You? You have limits. You can't lift a thousand pounds. Or turn water into wine. Or cause the seasons to change. All of us are limited by our finite reality. But God? He's absolutely limitless.

Shawna didn't believe that—and she told God as much as she walked through a particularly tough time in her marriage. Giving up seemed the only answer. Her husband was flawed. She was angry and hurt. And God? He wasn't anywhere to be seen. He didn't seem to be moving any mountains or performing any miracles.

But then something miraculous *did* happen—her heart began to change. Shawna opened herself up to the possibility that God could intervene, even in this seemingly impossible situation. And He did.

Funny how that works. As soon as she gave God room to move, He did. And He proved to Shawna, once and for all, that nothing is impossible.

Lord, I struggle to know what's possible and what isn't. So many things seem impossible, but You're bigger than all of them. Thank You, Jesus, that You can do the undoable and make the impossible possible! Amen.

Forget the Former Things

"Forget the former things; do not dwell on the past. See, I am doing a new thing! Now it springs up; do you not perceive it? I am making a way in the wilderness and streams in the wasteland."
Isaiah 43:18–19 niv

You wonder if God will ever change your situation. Day in and day out, things remain the same. And though you want to believe a miraculous turnaround is coming, in your gut you doubt it.

Reread today's scripture as you ponder the possibilities of change—both in your circumstances and your heart. The Creator of the universe is instructing you to forget the former things. What former things? The mistakes you've made. The horrible way people have treated you. The imperfections in your attitude. The times you fell short. That awful sickness you went through. The financial struggle you faced.

All of that is now in the past. Even what happened an hour ago. It's behind you now, and God wants you to forget about it. Don't dwell on it.

Why is He so eager to have you looking forward? Because He knows that yesterday will tie you in knots. Today, though, is a fresh new day, filled with possibilities.

Rest easy. A new thing is springing up! God is making a way for you.

Thank You for doing new things, Lord! I know my situation can change because You are the author of change! Amen.

If God Is for You

Surely the arm of the LORD is not too short to save, nor his ear too dull to hear.

ISAIAH 59:1 NIV

If you put an ad in the paper for a bodyguard, what sort of protector would you seek? What qualifications would he need to have? No doubt you'd want someone muscular and brave, willing to defend you at any cost.

You wouldn't hire any bodyguard incapable of peak performance.

Now think about God, your ultimate bodyguard. His arm is not too weak to save you. In other words, He's got strength to spare. He could take down a zillion enemies—an entire army, in fact! And His ear isn't deaf to your call. The Lord can hear the most quiet cry for help you can gasp out. There's not a single flaw in Him.

Now that you see how perfect He is for the job, does it bring peace to your heart? You can truly rest easy, knowing the ultimate bodyguard is watching out for you.

Whew! No one can mess with You, Lord! You can take them down in a hurry. If You are for me, who can be against me? No one! Amen.

Nothing Can Stop Him

"I know that you can do all things;
no purpose of yours can be thwarted."
Job 42:2 NIV

Most people who live along the coast have probably experienced a hurricane or two. They blow in with terrifying strength, taking down everything in their path. If you know the storm is headed your way, you're also keenly aware that nothing—short of a miracle—can stop it.

Now think about God's power. If a thousand hurricanes joined forces, barreling toward land, they wouldn't have an iota of the power God has. (The wind and waves bow to Him, after all!) If He's really that powerful, if absolutely nothing can stop Him from accomplishing what He sets out to do, then why do we worry? Why would we fret?

Nothing can stop your unstoppable God. Fear can't. Job loss can't. Health issues can't. Even a marital breakup isn't enough to stop Him. Like the eye in the center of the storm, He's the calm place you're seeking. So rest in Him. He can't be stopped. . .and He's moving on your behalf.

What power, Lord! It blows my mind to think about it! Nothing even comes close. And best of all, no power of hell can stop You. The enemy can try, but he's got nothing on You! Amen.

With God

Jesus looked at them and said, "With man this is impossible, but with God all things are possible."
MATTHEW 19:26 NIV

We look at situations and say, "It's impossible. There's no way." And you know what? That's true. In the natural realm, they are impossible. We try and try to figure things out, but we just can't. We struggle emotionally to wrap our heads around how the situation will end. Our stomachs in knots, we can't calm our thoughts. We wonder if we'll ever be able to settle down.

Just remember those two very important words: *with God.*

Add those two words to any situation, and guess what? All the things that once seemed completely impossible now appear within reach. Your faith increases. Hope rises to the surface. You dare to dream again. And once you do, peace invades the scene.

With God, you can overcome.

With God, you will find your way.

With God, eternity is within reach.

And with God. . .you will find rest for your soul.

That's it, Lord! I couldn't figure it out on my own, but now I see that I was never supposed to. Without factoring You in, I'm powerless. But with You in the picture, all things are possible. Amen.

Scripture Index

GENESIS
2:2–3. 44
2:3. 45
3:8. 26
3:19. 21

EXODUS
14:14. 36
26:1. 81
33:14. . . . . 24, 111
33:22. 82

DEUTERONOMY
6:5. 97

JOSHUA
1:9. 43
6:14. 71

1 SAMUEL
1:12–14. 66
8:3. 171

1 CHRONICLES
16:11. 126
29:11. 103

2 CHRONICLES
7:14. 180
20:17. 37

JOB
7:1. 20
15:31. 132
42:2. 187

PSALMS
3:5–6. 32
4:4. 134
4:8. 29
16:8. 108
16:11. 25
19:14. 123
23:1–2. 124
23:2. 10
23:3. 183
23:4. 167
27:4. 28
30:6. 105
33:20. 65
34:4. 41
34:8. . . . . 139, 141
37:7. . . . . 35, 38
40:4. 131
42:6. 136
46:10. 34
55:6. 79
62:1. 64
62:1–2. 104
62:2. 100
73:26. 144
90:14. 110

91:1–2. 119
91:4. 80
91:5. 101
92:1. 47
95:2. 87
96:3. 153
100:3. 168
103:12. 177
107:1–3. 140
111:2. 138
116:7. 84
118:24. 163
119:105. 73
127:1–2. 174
127:2. 19
139:3. 18
139:7–10. . . . . 77, 83
143:5. 137
143:7–10. 33
145:16. 148

PROVERBS
3:5. 130
3:24. 30
13:3. 93
16:24. 122
21:15. 172
24:19. 102

ECCLESIASTES
5:12. . . . . 31, 98

SONG OF SOLOMON
4:2. 142

ISAIAH
1:17. 173
6:1–2. 125
14:3–4. 169
26:3. . . . . 78, 129
30:15. 54
40:29. 94
43:18–19. . . . . 92, 185
46:12. 70
48:17. 128
54:10. 158
58:11. 113
58:13–14. 179
59:1. 186
63:13–14. 160

JEREMIAH
1:19. 116
6:16. 49
15:20. 117
17:21. 48
24:7. 57
31:25. 109
33:12. 164

JOEL
2:13. 56

AMOS
3:3. 52

MICAH
6:8. 50

Nahum

1:7. 143

Malachi

2:6. 51

Matthew

5:16. 22
6:27. 42
6:33. 178
6:34. 147
8:24. 99
11:28. 59
11:28–30. 9
11:29. 69
12:34. 123
13:15. 53
13:30. 88
14:25–29. 61
16:18. 118
17:20. 120
19:26. 188
24:14. 150
28:20. 116

Mark

6:31. 14
12:2. 68

Luke

1:37. 184
2:10. 152
2:19. 134

John

10:4. 168
14:6. 62
14:27. . . . . 40, 74
16:13. 127
16:31–33. 76
16:33. 114

Acts

1:8. . . . . 75, 95

Romans

1:16. 151
5:5. 182
8:6. 161
11:29. 12
15:13. 159

1 Corinthians

1:17. 146
8:6. 85
10:13. 91

2 Corinthians

2:7. 135
2:13–14. 154
4:8–9. 106
5:6–9. 165
9:8. 175
9:15. 13
12:9. 145

Galatians

1:10. 72
6:9–10. 96

Ephesians

3:20–21. 86
4:26. 29

Philippians
4:6–7 . . . 39
4:8 . . . 176
4:11–13 . . . 112

Colossians
3:17 . . . 17
4:6 . . . 121

1 Thessalonians
1:3 . . . 67

2 Thessalonians
1:6–7 . . . 170

2 Timothy
1:6 . . . 11
3:16 . . . 55

Titus
2:11–14 . . . 157

Hebrews
4:1–2 . . . 149
4:9–10 . . . 46
4:11 . . . 15
4:15 . . . 107
6:18–20 . . . 23
12:1 . . . 58
12:1–2 . . . 166

James
4:8 . . . 27
4:13–14 . . . 60

1 Peter
5:6–7 . . . 90
5:7 . . . 89

2 Peter
3:8–9 . . . 162
3:9 . . . 63

1 John
4:7–8 . . . 155, 181
4:16–17 . . . 133
4:18 . . . 16
5:4–5 . . . 115
5:19–20 . . . 156

Revelation
3:15–16 . . . 98